Expressive Therapy
with Elders and the Disabled:
Touching the Heart of Life

About the Author

Jules C. Weiss, MA, ATR, is a registered Art Therapist who has been practicing art therapy and counseling for over eight years, with a range of populations from children to elders who have physical and/or psychological disabilities. Mr. Weiss specializes in working with people who have extended illnesses, those in residential or long-term care settings, and people who are in physical and/or emotional crisis. He has lectured and held workshops throughout the United States and in Canada. He holds a Master's degree in Creative Arts Therapy and a Bachelor's degree in sociology. Currently, he is a consultant on therapeutic programs, holds private practice in counseling and art therapy, and works as an Art Therapist in a New Orleans hospital.

Expressive Therapy
with Elders
and the Disabled:
Touching the Heart
of Life

Jules C. Weiss, MA, ATR

MMB MUSIC, INC.
10370 PAGE INDUSTRIAL BOULEVARD
SAINT LOUIS, MISSOURI 63132
314 ● 427-5660

Expressive Therapy with Elders and the Disabled: Touching the Heart of Life has also been published as *Activities, Adaptation & Aging*, Volume 5, Numbers 1/2, May 1984.

The Haworth Press, Inc., 10 Alice Street, Binghamton, NY 13904-1580
EUROSPAN/Haworth, 3 Henrietta Street, London, England WC2E 8LU

Library of Congress Cataloging in Publication Data

Weiss, Jules C.
    Expressive therapy with elders and the disabled.

    Bibliography: p.
    Includes index.
    1. Aged—Mental health services. 2. Physically handicapped—Mental health services.
3. Arts—Therapeutic use. 4. Art therapy. 5. Nursing home care. I. Title.
RC451.4.A5W43   1984   618.97′689165   84-571
ISBN 0-86656-266-4
ISBN 0-86656-372-5 (pbk.)

Dedication

To all people who are searching for their true home.
May they find it within their hearts.

Expressive Therapy with Elders and the Disabled: Touching the Heart of Life

Activities, Adaptation & Aging
Volume 5, Numbers 1/2

CONTENTS

SECTION I:
EXPRESSIVE THERAPY TECHNIQUES AND CASE STUDIES

Acknowledgments

I thank my wife and daughter, Fay and Kirsten, for their patience and consideration as I spent days typing and working on this book.
I thank Lamont Ingalls for his unending editorial support and advice.
I thank Joseph K. Lack for his fine photographic assistance.
I thank Julie Padgett for her valuable help.
I thank Phyllis M. Foster for her great assistance.
I thank Rose Levine Gaylean, D.X. Ross, Geraldine G. Earp and the many others who encouraged me to continue in my work.
I thank my parents, Emil and Gerta Weiss, for their love and support.
I thank all the people I have worked with for sharing their lives with me.

I thank God for allowing me to write this book.

Preface

The area of art therapy, and creative arts therapy in general, has always had an important role in the therapy and treatment of disabled individuals. When Jules Weiss asked me to review his book, I cautiously entered into his domain as one who works in the area of both Geriatric Psychiatry and General Psychiatry. To most psychiatrists and mental health workers, art therapy and other creative arts therapies tend to be a rather vague and sometimes abstruse area since most of us are not quite certain of their therapeutic applications. For such individuals, this book provides an important supplement and fills a vacuum that has been created in that area. Not only are the chapters very elegantly written, but the patients literally come alive in this book through their creations and through Mr. Weiss's compassionate and empathic descriptions and interpretations. There is no one chapter that I believe can be criticized in regards to both its completeness and helpfulness for all of us working in the mental health area. The chapters illustrate what can really be done with those individuals who on one level appear to have been closed off from the world, but who, obviously, when the appropriate tools are used in the right hands, can communicate in a very creative manner.

I recommend this book to all of us who are interested in working with those who appear to be in the dark recesses of disability, isolated from the rest of humanity.

David Shraberg, MD
Clinical Assistant
Professor of Neurology and Psychiatry
Tulane Medical School
New Orleans, LA

Foreword

As long as man has breath, he communicates. His voice may be silent, his language may not be understood, but he is still a living soul with a story to tell. When the traumas of life are too great people may choose to withdraw into themselves or rail at the world about them. Finding a key that helps to unlock these defenses takes sensitivity and skill.

In this book, health-care workers will not only find new therapies to assist residents in long-term care settings but also will become aware of the sensitivity and understanding required to reach many who may seem at first to be unreachable. This task is a noble one and the rewards of personal satisfaction which it brings are great.

A considerable amount of progress has been made in the past years in meeting the physical needs of residents in long-term care facilities. It is not enough, however, to care *for* the body alone: it is essential to care *about* the whole person. Much needs to be done, therefore, to meet the social, emotional, psychological, and spiritual needs of residents.

While the methods shown in this book may be but one more step in improving the lives and care of residents, the underlying sensitivity of the worker to the resident is of the utmost importance in any interaction or care.

What is this book all about? It is a guide to help workers offer creative means of expression to residents and to sensitively interact with them on a person to person basis.

Each one of us has a tale to tell; a life to be lived. When all the stories have been told we will see it will have made a magnificent mosaic.

Jules Weiss is a very special man who has devoted himself to helping individuals express themselves through a variety of creative avenues by using his expertise in art therapy and his love for those with whom he works. In this book, Jules shares some of his life experiences and skills.

xvi EXPRESSIVE THERAPY WITH ELDERS AND THE DISABLED

Touching the Heart of Life

Sensitive, feeling, creative be-ing
From whence did you come?
Out of darkness - made light?
Out of pain - made well?
Out of rejection - made whole?

To see the strength and beauty in the aged
To sense the wellness and ability in the infirmed
To guide with singular tenderness the pen and pencil
   in the faltering hand
Toward newness and happiness
Is Jules

Mrs. Patricia A. Kinsella
Long-Term Care Consultant

Introduction

Elderly and disabled individuals often find themselves unable to successfully conduct their lives as they did in the past. When an individual enters such a time in his life, new choices and approaches must be sought. I call this time of life a "rite of passage": working through difficulties to a new lifestyle or attitude toward life. If appropriate and satisfactory changes are not made and personal issues not dealt with during this time, depression and illness can set in. This is a period in which a person often needs to reshape or reorganize his life, to find new alternatives and a deeper meaning in life.

During this time, elderly and disabled individuals will often want to assess their past, become aware of and involved in the present, and seek new ways to actualize their desires and wishes. New needs may arise due to physical changes such as illnesses, strokes, cancer, or accidents and because of emotional difficulties related to changes in lifestyle and/or loss of abilities. Expressive therapy can aid in fulfilling these psycho-social needs.

Currently, recreational diversions are offered to elderly and disabled people who live in long-term care settings, nursing homes, senior citizen apartment complexes, or who participate in senior centers and related programs, but little or no psycho-social therapy is commonly available. Thus, there is a need for group and individual therapeutic activities which promote creativity, self-expression, communication, and understanding of one's life. Expressive therapy can satisfy the individual's psycho-social needs by helping the person work through his "rites of passage," dealing with significant and conflicting issues and problems. It also helps the individual find enjoyment in life.

Expressive therapy uses a variety of verbal and nonverbal techniques for therapeutic intervention and self-growth. Some of these are: art, music, movement, creative games, drama, writing, and verbal interplay. A major focus within this book is art therapy. In the art experience (e.g., spontaneous painting, drawing, sculpting) a person's inner experiences are revealed in the art expression. The art product becomes a personal permanent record for the individual's contemplation. Through the art process, the individual encounters and becomes aware of conscious and unconscious thoughts, feelings, conflicts, and passions.

Expressive therapy is a flexible modality of therapy which can be used with a wide range of populations: the frail elderly, the bed-ridden patient, the disabled individual, and the senior citizen (elder). It is an excellent modality for those who have difficulty verbalizing or expressing feelings, or who are unable to speak. This approach enables individuals to discover and understand themselves through their creative expressions. Expressive therapy is an active thera-peutic approach oriented to meet the individual's changing and de-veloping needs. This form of activity encourages self-expression and understanding through the individual's relationship (communi-cation) with himself and with others.

By participating in spontaneous and theme-related expressive ex-periences, individuals share, uncover, and develop an understand-ing of their lives. Through expressive therapy, the individual en-counters and explores the conscious and unconscious aspects of the self and learns to examine his life. These experiences of the self may manifest verbally through discussions, or nonverbally through drawing, writing, sculpting, or other forms of self-expression. This creative experience is a sharing that often speaks deeper than words. It fosters a vibrant communicative relationship with oneself, others, and the world which further enables the individual to relate more deeply to his life. The expression can be a private experience be-tween a person and his art product, or the art work may be shared with others as the individual communicates feelings and thoughts which were touched during his art experience.

As the group therapist, during and/or following an expressive therapy experience, I aid participants in recognition of conscious and unconscious feelings and thoughts. This guides the individual to affirm and acknowledge his sense of self. At times, I ask partici-pants to verbally express their internal experience. I also may relate my feelings (in a non-threatening manner) about the participant's art and verbal expression as a way of giving support and assisting or en-couraging the individual to further express or acknowledge the self. Although my focus as an expressive therapist is on self-expression, it is also on learning to accept oneself and to deal effectively with all aspects of one's life.

The particular approach to expressive therapy discussed within this book is based on self-understanding, and on acceptance and love for oneself and others. A focus of this approach is to enable participants to uncover the truth of their lives. It allows individuals to realize their full potential by accepting themselves and creatively expressing their experiences of life. This approach facilitates the emergence of self-esteem and acknowledges the feelings and thoughts of the individual; thus, helping the person to experience a fullness in his life. It affirms that all people can feel accepted, loved, and cherished for who they already are.

This book is a compilation of several years of my work as a counselor and expressive therapist with elders and the disabled at various facilities (hospitals, institutions, senior citizens centers, adult day care programs, and mental health clinics). It describes experiences, case studies, insights into psycho-social dynamics, therapeutic techniques and processes in working with a variety of psychologically and physically disabled adults and elders, and minimally handicapped elders.

Each facet of this book is designed to illuminate the relevant issues and give direction to a therapeutic process which is sensitive to the needs of elders and the disabled. Meaningful issues facing elders and the disabled are explored, and some very important questions concerning therapy and personal growth for these populations are brought to light. Laymen and professionals can use and adapt the techniques and processes of expressive therapy to explore various therapeutic, emotional, intellectual, and spiritual depths. This book may be used as a reference for examples of therapeutic processes useful in working with elders and the disabled to improve the quality of their lives. All incidents discussed are true, but the names have been changed for confidentiality.

* * *

Throughout the text I have substituted the word elder for senior citizen or geriatric patient. The term is used in a dignifying manner, to note a person who deserves to have a sense of self-esteem, respect, and opportunities for a fulfilling life. This term is best defined by a statement made by Barry Barkin of the Live Oak Institute (© 1977) in Oakland, California.

Definition of an Elder

An Elder is a person who is still growing, still a learner, still with potential and whose life continues to have within it promise for, and connection to the future. An Elder is still in pursuit of happiness, joy, and pleasure, and her or his birthright to these remains intact. Moreover, an Elder is a person who deserves respect and honor and whose work it is to synthesize wisdom from long-life experience and formulate this into a legacy for future generations.

Expressive Therapy with Elders and the Disabled: Touching the Heart of Life

Section I:
Expressive Therapy
Techniques and
Case Studies

Chapter 1

Regression of the Hospitalized Elderly and Disabled Patient as Explored Through Art Therapy

PART I

Regression is an emotional, behavioral, and cognitive enactment of a return to a previous time in a person's life. People who are regressed often relive, in a compulsive manner, desires, feelings, thoughts, and actions from their past. Regression can be caused by organic problems (e.g., stroke, Korsakoff's syndrome), or may be induced by psychological problems (e.g., traumatic experiences, lack of nurturing), or by an impoverished environment. Regression can act as a maladaptive action in avoidance and denial of the present reality, or as an ego-sustaining activity in a physically, emotionally, and psychologically painful situation. This chapter will focus on the psychological causes and effects of regression and how this process is explored through art therapy.

The phenomenon of regression in institutional settings is often a major problem. Elderly and disabled people who live in institutions or hospitals often experience a loss of self-esteem, self-assurance, and integrity due to the loss of their independence and self-reliance, and a loss of significant relationships. These feelings of loss can induce withdrawn and isolative behavior which acts as a catalyst for further regression.

> Frustration of wishes and needs produce conflict and stress, which are the basic elements of neurosis; but the successful resolution of conflict is the basis of growth and development.[1]

Elderly and disabled individuals often have few opportunities for the resolution of personal conflicts within the institutional setting; there-

3

fore, maladaptive patterns of dealing with conflict and stress may appear, such as, withdrawal, isolation, and regression. These patterns of behavior are often seen in their nonverbal expressions.

A way of dealing with conflict and stress for regressed patients is seen in the nonverbal messages they give by clinging to their beds, blankets, pillows, or other people as they seek a means to express their need for consistency, validation, and relationship with others. Through holding onto and fixating upon certain types of behavior, patients are able to control, to a certain extent, the stimulus from their environment, helping them to feel a sense of self and personal power.

During my work as an expressive therapist at a long-term care/rehabilitative facility, I was able to perceive the regressional processes caused by organic impairments, psychological conflicts, and by the patients' social situations. Thus, the following therapeutic approach was structured to compensate for the tendencies of patients to regress and isolate.

I found that a patient's regressional process may be significantly lessened through a stimulating, nurturing, communicative, and interactive environment. The group art therapy experience gave patients a chance to express their feelings, thoughts, and concerns, and be recognized by themselves, their peers, and staff in an activity which counteracted the patients' regressional tendencies. Through this process, patients began to feel and act as individuals, expressing their feelings and thoughts, feeling proud of their activities and of themselves. They found that just being aware of and in communion with others gave significance to their lives.

The art therapy group consisted of from five to fifteen elderly and disabled participants, and was held at a round table in the day room. The sessions would begin by handing out art materials, putting on some lively music, and talking to the group about a theme they could explore through writing, drawing, or painting, individually or together. Patients were encouraged to share their feelings and thoughts with each other in order to bridge their isolation and develop a sense of community.

An important aspect of the art therapy process was for patients to uncover and discuss various personal, conflictual, and timely issues during the group activity. The recognition of the individuality and importance of each person is essential to the integrity of this process. Without this recognition, patients may begin to regress and isolate.

During the art therapy sessions described in the following pages (the cases of Mr. K, Mr. H, and Mr. B), aspects of the patients' regressional processes became apparent, and significant issues and concerns were brought up and addressed. By the aid of the art therapy process a sense of community, intimacy, personal recognition, and sharing was created within the group setting.

The Regressional Process as Noted with the Severely Handicapped-Regressed Patient.

In group art therapy sessions, I noticed that each person usually drew only within a small area in front of himself. However, the very confused patient would often draw outside this confined space because of difficulty in perceiving boundaries. Mr. K, a participant in the art therapy group, was a confused patient in his sixties whose medical diagnosis was senile dementia. In art therapy sessions which were focused on group murals he would scribble over other patients' writings and drawings as if he did not notice them (see Photo 1.1). He also scribbled randomly on any nearby object. His art activity could be compared to the description of a child's art expression in Rhoda Kellogg's book, *Analyzing Children's Art:* ''The Emergent Diagrams do not rely on the edges of the paper for definition, nor do they present clear shapes.''[2] This lack of boundary and image clarification is often characteristic of the very confused patient (see Photo 1.2).

In Mr. K's drawing style and picture (as with other regressed patients), a regression and fixation to childlike behavior is evident. His drawing style was comparable to that of the early stage of childhood in which children draw circular patterns by means of long arm movements. At this stage, children also produce sounds with the crayon or the art tool as an exploratory and sensory stimulus during the art activity. While he drew, Mr. K often made tapping noises with his felt-tip pen or crayon, feeling the texture of the paper, engrossed in the drawing experience. Mr. K was usually so involved in the task of drawing that he did not notice the people around him or the boundaries of the paper.

Mr. K's responses in art therapy typified his exploration of his surroundings in a ''regressive'' tactile and sensory mode: touching, tapping, and drawing on whatever was in reach. His art expression was his way to relate to the world in a manner that he could experience and feel acknowledged.

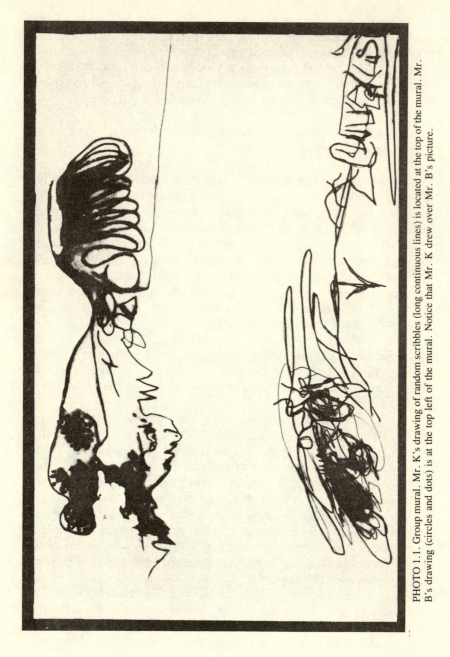

PHOTO 1.1. Group mural. Mr. K's drawing of random scribbles (long continuous lines) is located at the top of the mural. Mr. B's drawing (circles and dots) is at the top left of the mural. Notice that Mr. K drew over Mr. B's picture.

PHOTO 1.2. Mr. K's painting. Notice the lack of clear shapes and forms.

The Regressional Process as Noted with the Moderately Handicapped-Regressed Patient.

The symptoms of moderately handicapped-regressed patients may appear as a reflection of their uneasy feelings and thoughts toward their situation which they would like to deny, avoid, and forget. Patients often have much difficulty verbalizing these uneasy feelings and thoughts. Through the use of art therapy such feelings can be brought out in a nonverbal, nonthreatening manner and discussed openly.

I found that regressed elderly and disabled patients in the art therapy group who were not severely confused or disoriented displayed a need to control their environment. They rarely reached out to others, typifying the isolation found with these populations. The act of setting boundaries in their art expression is shown by a regimented style of drawing as seen on a representative group mural (see Photo 1.3). This confined drawing style, where each patient drew only within an enclosed area, symbolized their need for order and control. These patients would set increasingly rigid boundaries in their interactions and movements, as well as in their drawings.

Mr. H, a mildly regressed patient in his seventies, joined the weekly art therapy group. He was diagnosed by the doctor as having a mild case of senile dementia with schizoid tendencies. Mr. H had an obsessional craving for food, his bed, and companionship. At the beginning of the art therapy sessions he would sit stoically and silently, but after a few minutes of silence he usually blurted out a request in a loud, demanding, angry, almost pleading tone of voice, as if speaking to people who were ignoring him. He usually asked to either go back to his bed or to have something to eat.

In one of Mr. H's first art therapy sessions he drew expressionless faces with wandering eyes and no mouth (see Photo 1.4). This picture resembled, in an abstract way, two nurses and a staff doctor who worked on his ward. During a discussion of the drawing with Mr. H, I realized that his picture represented the feelings he often expressed about the staff. He felt the staff gave a seemingly empty display of concern for him and desire to help him. Whenever he mentioned this feeling he seemed to become quieter and more withdrawn. After he drew a picture in the art therapy session he would usually sit back and ponder it, looking more relaxed and at peace with himself. I felt at these times, through his art and writing, he had made a significant statement to himself, or acknowledged his feelings and felt recognized.

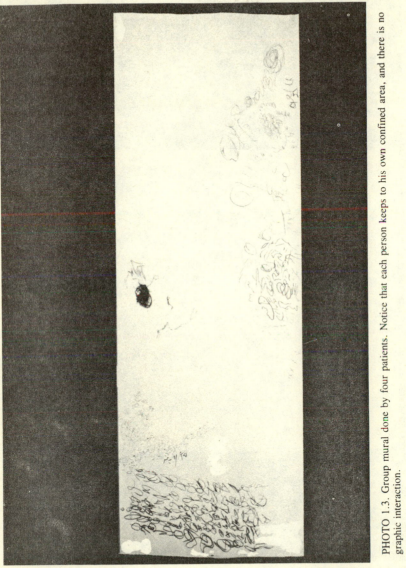

PHOTO 1.3. Group mural done by four patients. Notice that each person keeps to his own confined area, and there is no graphic interaction.

9

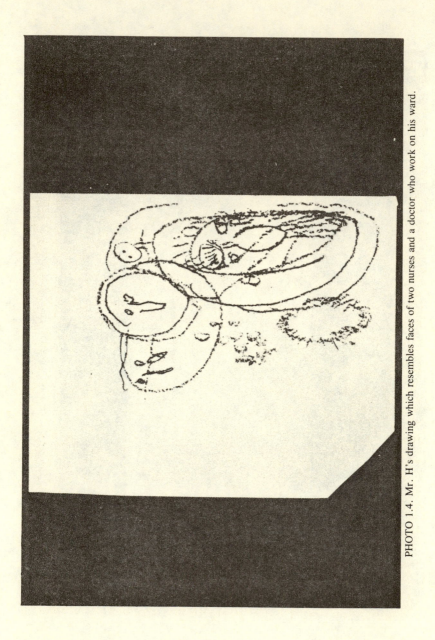

PHOTO 1.4. Mr. H's drawing which resembles faces of two nurses and a doctor who work on his ward.

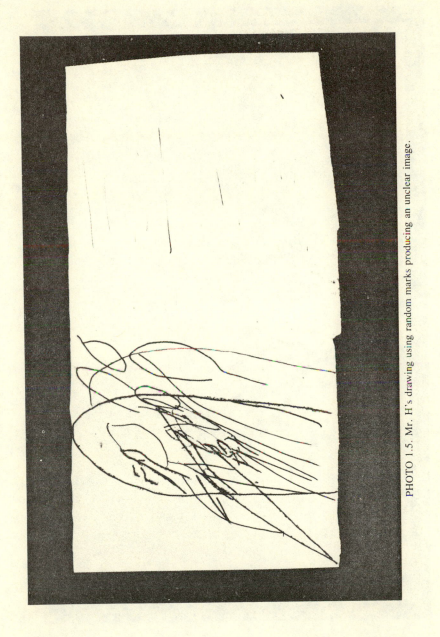

PHOTO 1.5. Mr. H's drawing using random marks producing an unclear image.

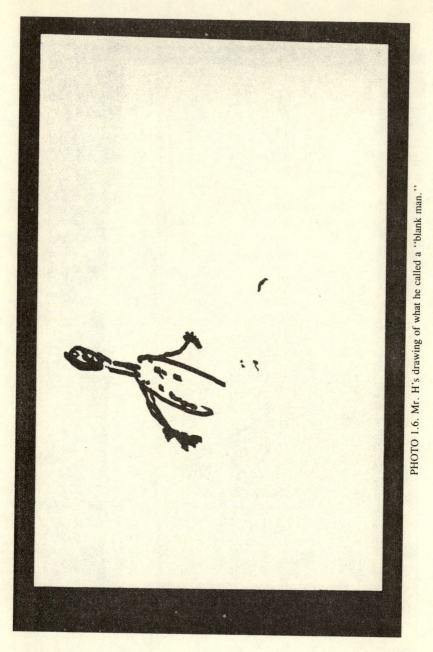

PHOTO 1.6. Mr. H's drawing of what he called a "blank man."

Mr. H often told me that he was lonely in the hospital. His obsessional demands could be seen as a regression to childlike behavior and as an attention-seeking request for nurturing, compassion, and relationship with others. The demands were primarily oral and tactile (as noted by his requests for food and touching) which are common with regressed patients. His requests signified a number of possible factors: the lack of sensory stimulus in the institutional setting, his feelings of isolation, loneliness, withdrawal, and unmet needs. Mr. H's behavior exemplified the tendency in patients to isolate due to their anger and frustration, thus reinforcing their regressional process. This process may also manifest as an obsessional craving for physical comfort, food, and caring.

At the next art therapy session, Mr. H drew a picture of lines in random order with no structure or theme (see Photo 1.5). When I asked him what he was drawing he exclaimed in a loud sharp voice, over and over, "This is nothing, nothing." At the end of the session he was in an angry, silent mood and wheeled his wheelchair into the ward, next to his bed. Later in the day, when he was in bed, I asked him how he was feeling. He replied in an angry tone, "I want to go home!" I said, "Isn't this your home?" He replied in an even angrier and louder voice, "What do you think, the way they treat me!" His words bit at my bones and I felt his pain and anguish.

Mr. H's anger was reflected in the way he acted, particularly in his obsessional pleading for favors. This was compounded by his negative attitude about living in an institution. For Mr. H the institution did not feel like his home, even though he would live there until he died. He seemed to find a sense of autonomy in his loneliness and anger—an autonomy in which he may be reaching back to his childhood for his memories, strength, and consolation.

In his third picture (see Photo 1.6) Mr. H portrayed the top half of a stick figure which he titled "blank man." The bleakness found in this drawing seemed to mirror his feelings of himself. A wheelchair patient, such as Mr. H, who draws a person without legs could be unconsciously denying that he has legs. There may be several reasons for this denial: he does not use them, he is embarrassed about his inability to use his legs, he may be denying that he has a problem with his legs, or other factors.

The randomness and incompleteness of his pictures reflected his frustrations. Mr. H's pictures illustrated a disjointed, confused feeling; he seemed to be saying that he could not put all of the pieces of his life together. His drawings displayed his anger, his need for love, his confusion about where he is, complicated by his wanting to be home. As Mr. H faced his drawings, he faced his life.

Mr. H's regressional process, like that of many patients in a similar situation, was aided by the fact that he felt his personal needs were not being met. In some cases, staff members may not recognize these needs and therefore are not helpful in offering opportunities for satisfying these personal needs. Due to Mr. H's frustration and feelings of isolation, he withdrew his communication and regressed in a manner that led him to focus in a compulsive way on his primary needs.

These issues began to be brought out and discussed through his drawings. In Mr. H's first drawing (see Photo 1.4) he portrayed the hospital staff as cold and stern. In his second and third drawings (see Photos 1.5 and 1.6) he revealed deeper feelings of confusion and emptiness. By recognizing his feelings in his art work he was able to verbalize his sense of loneliness and feeling lost within the hospital. In Mr. H's regressional process he may inwardly and outwardly be battling against the impersonal attitude of the institution, making a statement of his need for intimacy, nurturing, and concern. Many patients within the institutional setting give similar verbal and non-verbal statements in their own way. These statements, which are so often misread by others, are significant comments on the conditions of their life.

The Regressional Process as Noted with the Disabled Individual and the Minimally Handicapped Elder Patient

Regression with these populations can be either an adaptive form of regression to momentarily compensate for one's plight in life, or a regression that is defensive due to avoidance and/or denial of the present reality. For many elderly and disabled people, "the present may be bleak; the past, particularly in distorted, idealized form, often proves more gratifying."[3] How common this state of affairs is! For some individuals regression may be a black cave to hide in, especially for people who refuse to acknowledge the present and are not able to deal with reality. But, a regression to one's past when the individual felt his life was more fulfilling and enjoyable can be a healthy retreat. Because of physical pain and psycho-social stress, there may be times when regression may seem appropriate for an individual. It can be an alternative that we choose. This type of alternative is, at times, a healthy and adaptive avenue.

Mr. B, who was in his fifties, was a member of the art therapy group who showed signs of withdrawn and adaptive regressive behavior. Mr. B was a double-leg amputee, with one arm amputated below the elbow. He had a long history of alcoholism and poor self-care.

In many of Mr. B's drawings (see Photos 1.7 and 1.8) he drew primarily food items, although he sometimes drew objects that he would have at parties or "friendly gatherings" in his past, such as cards and dice. When I asked him why he mainly drew food, he said, "That is all I think of, that is all I know." In the past he was a cook, but he rarely spoke of his previous work, only of food. At times the topic of sexuality would come up and he expressed frustration and embarrassment in wanting to masturbate but feared being caught by a nurse.

Mr. B's focus on oral gratification can be seen as a sublimation of sexual and ego-gratifying drives and needs and a regression to an oral dependency. As a replacement for unmet personal needs and desires within his institutional life, Mr. B focused on food in a compensatory manner.

Mr. B emerged as a leader in the art therapy group, discussing his feelings and thoughts, and sharing his humor. In Mr. B's sixth art therapy group session he began to draw animals and other objects, while still including food items in all of his pictures. By including new and different objects in his drawings, Mr. B was symbolically representing his gradual incorporation of more activity. This activity encompassed a new wide spectrum of thoughts and social interactions in his life. At this time he was also less obsessed with drawing and talking about food items and would discuss other topics. Through his drawings and discussions he was able to recall memories of his past, discuss daily events in his life, and share feelings and thoughts in an intimate manner with fellow patients and staff. This process enabled Mr. B to feel acknowledged and appreciated within the context of his setting.

In the institutional setting Mr. B felt isolated, just another patient, another part of the "furniture" in a large complex; the art therapy experience gave him a sense of himself as a member of the community in which he lived. His further development of self-esteem was seen by his increasing conversations and interactions with patients and staff. He became less self-centered and spent more time interacting with others in his environment, creating new relationships and doing new and different things. Mr. B's participation in

PHOTO 1.7. Mr. B's drawings representing food objects such as doughnuts and coffee.

PHOTO 1.8. Another example of Mr. B's drawing of food objects.

the group art therapy experience made a significant difference in the way he acted and cared about himself and others, helping him to focus on his present reality and find enjoyment there.

PART II

The Regressional Process and Related Issues in the Institutional Setting.

Patients who live in long-term care settings are often consciously and/or unconsciously looking for surrogate relationships to substitute for the pain and loss of intimacy and caring within their life. For these reasons, the patient is drawn toward a passive symbiotic relationship with his or her primary caretaker.

> The dependency pattern is one woven not purely out of the "incapacities" or innate lack of self-reliance of the individual, but also of the social tolerances and intolerances which encourage or make necessary resort to dependent demands.[4]

In the institutional setting, the elder and disabled person's major relationship is usually with his primary caretaker, a nurse or orderly. There are direct parallels between the patient-staff and the infant-mother relationship. In both, the main concern is primarily over food and physical comfort. Since it may be difficult for the hospital staff to have an emotionally significant relationship with the patient which is intimate, meaningful, and nurturing, those individuals needing this type of relationship may become depressed and isolated.

The hospital staff most often deals with the patient's physical condition and may overlook the emotional trauma and needs of this time in the patient's life. The emotional support, love, and intimacy which is found with family and friends is a component of a positive, healthy, and healing way of life. Although such nurturing is an essential aspect of long-term health care, it is not always provided in the nurse/patient relationship. This need for nurturing brings up the question: How can the hospital staff truly aid the patient in such a need? The answer to this question is a creative, loving relationship, which each health-care worker, treatment team, and institution needs to mutually discover and examine.

Regressional Correlatives

There are several issues which contribute to the regressional process of the patient within the institutional setting. One of these issues, a fear of intimacy, may appear in conjunction with the patient's lessening of self-esteem and confidence. When a patient moves into a hospital he may experience a confusion and lack of security relative to his self-image and place in life. Patients who are suddenly hospitalized, or placed in a long-term care setting with people they do not know, are confronted by many new experiences, conflicts, and personal issues such as: facing the fact of one's own mortality by the recognition that other patients (their peers) are sick and dying; taking a risk in becoming intimate with someone who may die and leave the person with a feeling of personal loss; and living in an environment where most relationships and activities are generally superficial.

I have known patients in hospitals and long-term care settings who did not even acknowledge the person in the bed next to them. This was the patient's way of denying the reality of living in the hospital or institution. These were people who lived in their pasts, in dreams, and who hoped constantly that the present was just a nightmare that they would wake from and find themselves back home again. This type of denial of the environment often brings about regression.

Other major issues for the institutionalized and hospitalized patient in relation to his environmental setting and milieu are trust vs. mistrust, intimacy vs. isolation, and autonomy vs. shame and doubt.* These issues are especially crucial to elderly and disabled patients in their transition to living in a long-term care setting or hospital. Such issues continue to be significant in the developmental conflicts inherent in adjusting to living in this new environment.

Trust vs. Mistrust

In the issue of trust vs. mistrust, the patient faces ambivalence towards and conflict over trusting the environment he lives in, the people he socializes with, and the staff he depends upon. An individual in any new situation has to first deal with this most basic of

---

*The noted issues are also cited as developmental milestones by Erik Erikson in *Identity and The Life Cycle*.

issues. Therefore, it may be very difficult for the patient to form satisfying relationships and to feel comfortable in a new setting. The issue of trust vs. mistrust is crucial for the patient who must acclimate to living in a hospital or institution, develop new relationships with fellow patients and staff, and deal with physical illnesses and the emotional strain of this abrupt change in environment. Patients wishing to adjust and feel comfortable in a new setting may have difficulty with various factors, such as: creating a meaningful, intimate, and satisfying rapport with fellow patients and staff; adjusting to a new routine; becoming accustomed to having other people (nurses, orderlies, activity therapists, and doctors) designate their activities; and other factors which contribute daily to their well-being.

Intimacy vs. Isolation

The issue of intimacy vs. isolation becomes paramount within the institutional setting when the patient recognizes the need for meaningful relationships and intimacy in his new environment. A patient's fear of intimacy may have been conditioned by psychological and emotional traumas due to being disabled, ill, or old (e.g., feeling different from others, having low self-esteem, feeling unproductive).

A patient can be experiencing a fear of isolation and a fear of intimacy simultaneously. The isolated patient may feel depressed and very lonely. However, if the patient wishes to be intimate with someone, there are other conscious and unconscious fears which the patient may face, such as: the fear of rejection; the fear of getting too close to someone and possibly being emotionally hurt; the fear of losing a friend who may die; the fear of becoming too attached to life in the hospital, consequently not wanting to leave to go back to his previous home. These fears can be a haunting, daily experience of unfulfilled personal needs.

Autonomy vs. Shame and Doubt

Another issue of major importance for the patient living in an institutional setting is autonomy vs. shame and doubt. The need to feel autonomous is a basic element of personal freedom and psychological health. For an elderly and disabled patient who realizes that he cannot do things as well as he did in the past, the fear of failure, of making mistakes, of criticism, and of being rejected for one's actions as an individual are paramount concerns. The feeling of help-lessness, without a sense of autonomy, can be a devastating feeling for the patient. But, for the individual who wants to exhibit autonomy and independence, the thought of failure in his actions can beget shame and doubt, and be just as terrifying. Resolving the issue of autonomy vs. shame and doubt is a major milestone in the development of an individual's self-esteem and ability to function independently.

Although autonomous activity can be very healthy and esteem-building for the patient, the verbal and nonverbal messages staff sometimes relate to the patient does not support his sense of autonomy. He is told to not step out of the normal hospital procedure or milieu and to let the staff take care of him. This message implies that it is better for the staff to do an activity for the patient than for the staff to wait for the attempts of the patient, especially when the possibility exists that the patient may fumble in his or her efforts. A patient does not want to be taken care of like an object, but wants to be seen as an individual who can exhibit a sense of autonomy and self-care.

In the family/patient relationship a double standard is often applied. Although it is acceptable for family members to have the patient go through rehabilitation and learn new skills, they often do not like to see the patient struggle, so they will do the needed tasks for the patient. This pattern impedes rehabilitation by reinforcing the patient's negative self-image and lack of confidence. This is not to negate the sympathetic qualities of helping others, but to question whether in a specific situation these qualities are beneficial or detrimental. At times, sympathy, consolation, and physical help by the family (and/or staff) can negate a patient's strength, integrity, and qualities as an able person. This situation is comparable to an over-protective mother who acts out of her need to give, dominate, and/or control the child. It is the author's belief that it is better to teach patients a skill they need or want to learn, rather than doing the task for them. Of course, there are exceptions to this situation, but an awareness of when to teach a skill and when to help perform the task is necessary.

A person who "helps people" in an over-zealous or time-saving manner may actually be crippling a person by doing his tasks for him. These "helping" actions can create overdependency and take away the individual's initiative to try to take new steps in growth and responsibility. Patients do not want to be smothered by kindness, but want to be able to feel that they are persons who have a sense of autonomy and can give to others. *All people* can share their love, thoughts, and feelings in many different ways. Patients feel degraded when they are only given to, as children are, and not offered the opportunity to also give and share.

A beneficial therapeutic relationship between the family/staff and the patient involves aiding the patient in recognizing his situation, noting problems, difficulties, strengths, and offering the patient a choice of possible alternatives and an opportunity to share his feelings and thoughts. The family/staff can work with the patient to assist in creating and acting on alternatives and inspire the patient toward health and well-being. It is this family/staff and patient process which motivates the patient toward continued health, healing, and happiness.

It is difficult enough for an elderly or disabled person to take the risk of acting autonomously when his self-esteem is already low due to a negative self-image. If the staff and family members truly want to help an individual, they will take the time to teach the patient new skills to help him live more independently and encourage him to share his feelings and thoughts with others so that he may continue to grow emotionally, physically, and spiritually.

CONCLUSION

A hospital or institution is seldom similar to a home: the place in which people find support for their health and happiness. The hospital environment is based on the medical model of treating people in a sterile environment until they are well enough to go home. However, for those long-term patients who may reside in an institution or hospital for a good portion of their lives, a vital part of their treatment needs to be the creation and maintenance of a healthy daily life. This includes having a sense of home and security, developing relationships with others, and participating in invigorating and interesting activities.

To illustrate this need—in a long-term care setting, the administration insisted that I take down the patients' drawings and paintings that were hanging by the patients' beds. Their reasoning was that the tape on the back of the pictures might damage the paint on the walls and they would then have to repaint the ward. They would not consider using a different type of tape that would not damage the paint. At that moment, the administration felt that the paint on the walls was more important than the patients' self-esteem, sense of pride and feelings of achievement. (They wanted to display the pictures on a bulletin board which was clearly visible to guests and visitors. However, the bulletin board was down a hall that most patients did not go through.) The art expression of the patients was a display of their ability to express themselves and a recognition of their individuality. By not allowing the patients to have their pictures displayed by their bedside, the administration was disregarding the patients' feelings, thoughts, and need for a supportive environment.

> In order to maintain his self-esteem he may crave appreciation, marks of affection, or reassurance that he has made an impression upon the world in his lifetime. Through his words, his deeds, or through his children.[5]

The need for dignity and pride in oneself and in one's accomplishments is essential, especially for patients who are going through serious life changes and making major adjustments. A patient's regression may be a natural response to an environment where there is a lack of individuality, nurturing, self-expression, sense of accomplishment, intimate relationships, motivating experiences, and opportunities for learning and growth.

Because intimate relationships and fulfilling activities are often lacking for the institutionalized elderly and disabled patient, the individual may have nowhere to focus his attention and conversation but on the past. This focus can breed regression, isolation, and loss of contact with reality. This is the opposite of personal growth, the opposite of a rehabilitative experience. We need to recognize the responsibility we have to take care of and provide for patients as we would want to be aided, by offering opportunities for growth, learning, and sharing.

NOTES

1. Pollak, O. *Social Adjustment in Old Age.* New York: Social Science Research Council, 1948, page 45.

2. Kellogg, R. *Analyzing Children's Art.* California: Mayfield Publishing Company, 1970, page 35.

3. Jackel, M. A. "Senescence." In G. Wiedman (Ed.), *Personality Development and Deviation.* New York: International Universities Press, Inc., 1975, page 440.

4. *Toward Better Understanding of Aging.* Seminar on Aging. Aspen, Colorado: Council on Social Work Education, 1954, page 43.

5. Ibid., page 23.

BIBLIOGRAPHY

Brenner, C. *The Elementary Textbook of Psychoanalysis.* New York: Doubleday, 1974.

Erikson, E. *Childhood and Society.* New York: W. W. Norton and Company, 1950.

————*Identity and the Life Cycle.* New York: W. W. Norton and Company, 1980.

Jackel, M. A. "Senescence." In G. Wiedman (Ed.), *Personality Development and Deviation.* New York: International Universities Press, Inc., 1975.

Kellogg, R. *Analyzing Children's Art.* California: Mayfield Publishing Company, 1970.

Klein, M. *Contributions to Psycho-Analysis. 1921-45.* New York: McGraw-Hill, 1964.

Kubler-Ross, E. *Death: The Final Stage of Growth.* New Jersey: Spectrum Books, 1975.

Madison, P. *Freud's Concepts of Regression and Defense, Its Theoretical and Observational Language.* Minneapolis: University of Minnesota Press, 1961.

Pollak, O. *Social Adjustment in Old Age.* New York: Social Science Research Council, 1948.

Sarbin, T. *Studies in Behavior Pathology.* New York: Holt, Rinehart and Winston, 1962.

Strachey, J. *The Standard Edition of the Complete Works of Sigmund Freud.* London: Hogarth Press, 1963.

Thompson, C. *Psychoanalysis: Evolution and Development.* New Jersey: Thomas Nelson and Sons, 1950.

Toward Better Understanding of the Aged. Seminar on Aging - 1958. Aspen, Colorado: Council on Social Work Education, Inc., 1959.

Chapter 2

Creative Arts Therapy
for Various Elder Populations:
Techniques and Processes

> I wanted the healing process to grow out of the patient's own personality, not from suggestions by me that would have only a passing effect.
>
> C.G. Jung

Everything we do reflects our feelings, thoughts, and ideas. The way we move, what we write and draw, how we interact with others is all in reference to our feelings and thoughts. An individual's creative expression may tell of a personal situation, lend inspiration, or give a new perspective. For example, in the art and writing creative process the individual initially communicates with himself through the privacy of a written or drawn expression. The person then has the choice of sharing these feelings and thoughts with others.

Often the creative process enables a person to uncover aspects of the self that are blocked from conscious sight. The creative activity then becomes an inner and outer reflection of the self, expressing the conscious and unconscious. Through a therapeutic creative arts program, individuals may experience a closer communication with themselves and others, work through problems and issues, and find channels for their feelings, thoughts, and creative inspirations.

In providing therapy for the elderly, an approach which is exclusively verbal has many restrictions. Verbal psychotherapy is often a difficult modality of therapy for elders because the discussion of feelings and problems may seem taboo to them. Counseling and therapy have negative connotations for some elders.* They may feel these terms denote a person who is mentally ill and needs help. The bias which some elders may have against therapy may preclude them from seeing therapy as a way to deal with conflictual issues, to gain new tools in living, and to learn to live a happier, more fulfilling life.

People who have speech difficulties, and those who are mildly to severely regressed, are often unable to relate to and obtain aid from a cognitive, verbal psychotherapeutic process. A therapy which includes verbal, nonverbal, and sensory modalities is often more appropriate. Creative arts therapy,** which involves a variety of such modalities, is an excellent adjunctive or primary mode of therapy for elders and the disabled. It can be used with physical therapy, occupational therapy, speech therapy, and psychotherapy.

Elders who are not verbal (i.e., aphasic, regressed, withdrawn, or depressed) can find satisfaction in expressing their feelings and thoughts in a nonverbal but concrete manner through writing, drawing, and other creative arts modalities. For elders who are verbal, creative arts therapy can be used to further uncover, explore, and clarify their feelings and thoughts. The expressive therapist uses a wide range of tools, techniques, processes, and opportunities to assist elders to express, acknowledge, explore, and deal with the subject matter of their lives.

For the purpose of obtaining a clearer insight into the issues, concerns, and particular creative arts therapy activities for elders, I have divided the elder population into three categories. These categories are based on cognitive awareness, physical and emotional limitations and abilities, range of communicative skills, and the ability to perform activities of daily living skills. The categories are:

A. The Minimally Handicapped Elder Population—cognitively alert and able to communicate.
B. The Moderately Handicapped-Regressed Elder Population—uncertain of person, place, and time: possibly vacillating in and out of reality.

---

*I have seen a better response by elders to creative arts therapy sessions when it is called "creativity in self-development" to avoid the stigma of the term therapy (this is a subjective issue which would vary with the client population, milieu, and facility).

**Throughout the book the terms expressive therapy and creative arts therapy are used almost interchangeably. I use the term creative arts therapy to specifically refer to art, movement, and music therapy. Expressive therapy is a more general term to signify these three modes of therapy and other nonverbal and verbal modalities of creative therapy.

C. The Severely Handicapped-Regressed Elder Population—
having a lack of boundaries and a confused sense of person,
place, and time.

I have developed several creative arts therapy activities which are
designed to meet the particular therapeutic needs of each group.
These activities are described later in this chapter.

One of the major needs of elders is acceptance, both personally
and by the community or facility in which they live. This is especially true at this sensitive time, when they are adjusting to major life
changes and finding a new sense of self. Some of the more general
goals elders may have are:

1. To rediscover the personal meaning of their inner and social
   lives.
2. To use their available interpersonal tools to promote interaction and communication with others.
3. To develop a healthy sense of ego strength.
4. To stimulate their intellectual, physical, and emotional faculties which can aid toward the fulfilling of their potential.
5. To review their lives and their personal perspectives, and to
   give further insight into how their personal choices impact
   their ways of living; to come to terms with conflicting and
   negative feelings; and to see the value of their individual lives.
6. To feel a "wholeness in one's being"; to create a personal outlook of fulfillment and meaning in life.

CREATIVE ARTS THERAPY PROCESS

The creative arts therapy process contains many components.
Two major aspects of this process are the developing relationship
between the client and therapist and the relationship the client has
with his creative process. The development of trust, acceptance, and
good faith between the client and therapist aids in honest and open
communication. This relationship can be fertile ground for the client's growth, which can then transfer to other relationships.

In creative arts therapy sessions, the therapist must suit the therapeutic modality and process to the person and situation. In this regard, the therapist needs to determine the following aspects of a
therapy session: which media is most appropriate (e.g., clay, drawing, painting), the setting, the use of group or individual sessions,

the structure of the activity, the use of music, and other variables relevant to the therapy session. A step-by-step outline for the use of creative arts therapy techniques is not given because the author feels that creative arts therapy sessions must be created from the needs of the situation and not from a preordained recipe.

Clients may sometimes resist doing art work or creative expression in certain media because they feel it is too childish. I have found it to be important to describe to participants the value of self-expression through art. In my work I emphasize to clients that the type of tool used for creative expression implies no judgment on the individual, but rather assists each person to feel at ease in relating to and expressing feelings and thoughts.

In creative arts therapy sessions, I often use background music and suggest a theme for clients to explore. These themes help participants to focus on, uncover, and communicate deep-seated feelings and thoughts. The use of themes may also help participants to momentarily experience and communicate the critical times and feelings of their lives. Through this process, participants may re-examine and re-evaluate their lives, finding a new sense of understanding and peace.

A. THE MINIMALLY HANDICAPPED ELDER POPULATION

The minimally handicapped elder population consists of elders who may have physical and/or emotional disabilities because of the natural processes of aging, or from illnesses or accidents. People in this group may be experiencing emotional crisis due to serious changes in their lives, such as, loss of intimate relations or changes in their self-identity. The role of creative arts therapy with this population is to foster creative expression; to promote socialization and meaningful dialogue; to express and deal with feelings and problems; to aid in re-examining the elders' lives and processes; to help elders relate to their sense of community; and to develop feelings of self-integrity and self-esteem.

Creative Arts Therapy Themes, Techniques, and Processes for the Minimally Handicapped Elder Population.

1. *Scribble drawing*—Have participants scribble in one or multiple colors, using a variety of lines, on a large piece of paper (eighteen inches by twenty-four inches is a recommended size). Once the

scribble is completed, participants should color in the picture to ex-
aggerate the feeling or image they see in the scribble. Then, ask the
participants to turn their pictures around to see the different views of
their drawing. This change of perspective may bring up other ideas
and feelings. When participants finish the task they can reflect on
their pictures, discussing what they may represent, what the pictures
remind them of, and how the art work makes them feel. Background
music may be helpful in the creative aspect of this activity.

Benefits—This is a loosening up activity. Spontaneous drawing can
be an avenue to explore feelings and thoughts brought up by the free
association or symbolic interpretation of the drawing. This is especially useful as a non-threatening beginning activity to foster discussion in a group setting.

2. *Time Line*—Have the participants draw time lines of their lives
(from the point of birth to now), marking the major points of growth
and significant incidents with words and drawings. Participants can
also list future events on their time line if they want to note possible
goals.

Benefits—This activity provides discussion and insight into the
meaningful experiences of life and the significance each experience
holds or can hold for the individual.

3. *Theme-related art expression*—Using various art media (e.g.,
painting, drawing, and sculpting), have participants explore feelings
and thoughts concerning aspects of their lives. The themes can be
related to family, friends, places they have been to, homes they have
lived in, or other past and present experiences.

Benefits—This activity helps to initiate discussion which explores
conscious and unconscious aspects of the participants' lives. It is
useful for group discussion and fosters the sharing of meaningful experiences.

4. *Draw a picture of your family (including yourself and all members of your family) and on a separate piece of paper draw a picture
of your ideal family.* The representation of the family can be an
abstract, symbolic, or realistic picture. The participants do not have
to draw, but can use cut-out pictures from magazines or shapes of
colored paper to define the family members.

Benefits—In this exercise it is important to discuss how the participants view the different members of their families, and their
place in the family structure. It is also valuable to discuss what the
participants feel they need to foster in their ideal families, to look at
what they are not currently receiving emotionally from their families, and to discover how to create and develop their ideal families.

5. *Draw a place you really want to be, doing an activity you especially want to do, with the person you most want to be with.* This drawing can be done with a variety of art materials, whatever media is most suitable for participants.

Benefits—This activity enables participants to explore and express where they long to be (or would like to go) and what their favorite activities are. It will also give participants a chance to share and discuss about an important person in their lives.

6a. *Group mural*—This task can be organized by participants. The group needs to decide on a theme, the materials to be used, and where the mural will be placed when it is finished. It is advisable to frame the group mural and hang it in a public place. The mural can be a multi-media project. Various materials may be used, such as, paints, felt-tip markers, beads, or cut-out pictures.

Benefits—The group mural activity fosters group process, group cohesion, and individual and group creativity. It is an enjoyable and meaningful activity for elders to work on together. The group mural can make a valuable statement about the participants' feelings and thoughts.

6b. *Group-story mural game*—Divide participants into two groups (group A and group B), each group optimally having four to eight people. Direct the groups to meet in a separate area so each group will not hear what the other group is planning. Each group will decide on a setting and activity or event they would like to draw together. On the group mural, each member is to draw himself performing an activity, and contribute to the overall drawing of the mural. The participants can only draw themselves and the scenery. Have both groups draw their respective mural without letting the other group see the mural and without talking about the meaning of the mural. After the murals are finished (use approximately twenty to thirty minutes for drawing the mural) have one group come to see the other group's mural and guess who the people in the mural are, what they are doing, and the overall theme of the picture. This activity can be made into a contest by giving one point to each group for every correct answer and taking away one point for every wrong answer. The group with the most points wins.

Benefits—This is a fun activity which aids in group building and promotes communication, socialization, and discussion.

7a. *Self-portrait*—An abstract or realistic self-portrait which includes words and cut-out pictures or drawings of important aspects of the participants' current lives.

Benefits—This activity allows participants to express and explore a personal view of themselves and their present lives. It may be important for participants to verbally express their feelings about their pictures and for the therapist to share his interpretation and feelings. Through this sharing, a common understanding of the meaning of the picture and the experience of the client can develop between the therapist and participant.

7b. *Self-portrait including important memories about one's past.* These pictures should include significant feelings and activities from the participants' past lives. The pictures can be abstract or realistic and may include a combination of drawings, cut-out pictures, and written words.

Benefits—This activity helps participants become in touch with important personal experiences from their pasts which may still have an influence in their present lives.

8. *Relaxation with guided imagery and deep breathing, followed by spontaneous drawing and/or painting.* This activity should be conducted in a room that has little or no disturbance from others outside of the group. While performing the relaxation techniques, the lights should be dimmed and soft background music may be played. Following the relaxation process (which can take from eight to twenty-five minutes), the participants should draw or paint their feelings and thoughts.

Benefits—This exercise enables participants to express intimate and deep feelings and thoughts while in a relaxed state of mind and body.

9. *Journal*—Have the participants make a journal to include their daily writings, drawings, and other important material. Each participant should also design a cover for their journal.

Benefits—This process enables participants to daily express their feelings and thoughts in a private and special way through the use of a personal diary. It allows them to record, examine, and reflect upon their lives. In this manner the participants can review the value, meaning, and feelings connected with their lives.

10. *Creative writing*—Ask the participants to write prose, poetry, stories, or poems, either fictional or autobiographical. The participants can share their writings through a group reading or publishing their writings in a newspaper produced by the creative writing group. Group discussions, following a public reading of the participants' writings, is a very important aspect of the therapeutic process in this exercise.

Benefits—Expressing, reflecting upon, recognizing and sharing feelings, thoughts, and important memories, are valuable benefits derived from this process.

11. *Movement*—Set up a movement group to stimulate and exercise the body and release stored-up energy and feelings. Design the group to accommodate any physical limitations of the participants. Use background music which reflects the participants' varied interests. The group leader can use a combination of sitting and standing exercises and movement patterns to insure safety for those participants who may be a little uncertain of their stability or who become easily tired. Dance patterns can be integrated into the movement exercises. In this activity it is helpful to teach massage techniques to aid participants in learning to relax.

A recommended reference book for exercises is *Be Alive As Long As You Live,* available from Preventicare Publications, c/o Lawrence Frankle Foundation, Charleston, West Virginia 25301.

Benefits—The movement (kinesthetic) process itself is a major benefit. It provides for exercising the body from head to toe; being in touch with the body and how it feels; moving to music and having a joyful group experience. This exercise can help to improve circulation, proper breathing, and can relax tense muscles.

12. *Music*—Have the participants play various instruments and create songs and games with different rhythms, beats, and words. Participants can play different parts of a song, harmonizing, improvising, and creating new melodies. They may enjoy playing and singing some of their favorite songs and developing a rhythm band. Recommended references are texts on Orff-Schulwerk.

Benefits—This is a valuable and fun group experience. Participants have the opportunity to relate to and express themselves with rhythm and beat, and to see how they can create music. There are several experiences and exercises which can be done in conjunction with listening to and playing music, such as, reality orientation, reminiscence, group interaction, deep and proper breathing, and other forms of learning.

13. *Puppet show*—Have elders put on a puppet show for other groups, such as children or families. The participants can design and make the puppets from papier-maché and other materials. Be creative and have the participants act out their parts with and without the hand-puppets. Participants may want to expand their drama and acting talents and put on a play, or a group of short skits.

Benefits—This activity provides an arena for socialization, creativity, and fun. It is a valuable learning experience which aids in the development of self-esteem and integrity through performing and giving to others.

The next few activities listed are not primarily creative arts therapy processes, but are activities which I have found to be effective and valuable in my work with minimally handicapped elders.

14. *Goal Mandala*—Draw the following illustration.

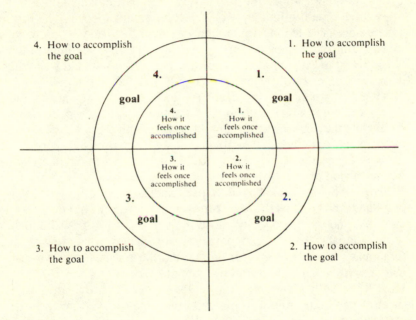

Each participant writes or draws four short-term goals they want to achieve. On the outside of the circle have the participants write how they can obtain the goal (by what method or action). Within the inner circle the participants will write how they think they will feel upon obtaining their goals.

Benefits—This is an excellent activity for short-term goal setting and evaluation. It is also very useful for insight into long-term goals and ways a person can achieve them.

15. *Dream-reality gift game*—Have the participants take a sheet

of paper and fold it in half. Ask them to think about and decide on the three gifts they want most in life. (The gifts can be objects or feelings, imaginary or real, things they may only dream of getting or things they are expecting.) The participants should then think about three people from whom they would like to receive the gifts. On one side of the paper have the participants write the name of each gift and draw a picture of it. The name of the person from whom they would like to receive the gift should be written next to each picture.

On the other half of the paper have the participants write and draw three dream gifts they would like to give someone. The gifts can be objects or feelings, imaginary or real: gifts they would want to give someone if they had the opportunity to give anything in the world. Next to each picture of a gift the participants should write the name of the person to whom they would like to give the gift.

After the group has completed the task, the participants should take about ten minutes each to read the gifts to the group, to name the people they chose to give to and receive from, and to show and explain their drawings to the group. After each participant shares his list with the group, a discussion should follow concerning the meaning and value of each gift.

Benefits—This exercise provides participants with a means to express and discuss what they want most in life, from whom they want the gifts, and the reason they chose the particular gifts. Additionally, participants have the opportunity to discuss what they wish (imaginary or real) to give to others and the reasons they want to give a particular gift to a specific person.

16. *"Who really knows me?"* game—Have each participant take a sheet of paper and fold it in half. On one side of the paper ask the participants to write "likes" and tell them they will be writing five objects or feelings they like. On the other side of the paper ask the participants to write "dislikes" and tell them that they will be writing five objects or feelings which they dislike. Then instruct the participants to list the "likes" and "dislikes" which they feel that others in the group do not know about. Caution the participants to not let anyone else see what they wrote. When the participants have completed their lists, have them write their names and favorite color on the paper. At the completion of this task have the participants fold their papers in half and give them to the group leader.

The group leader will collect the papers and prior to reading the lists aloud, the leader tells the participants, "when you hear your list read, pretend the list was written by someone else in the group." After the reading of each paper, the group must guess and vote on who they think it is. Subsequent to the group vote, the leader will read the favorite color of the individual, and then the group will vote again. After the second vote, the group leader will identify the writer of the paper and ask the individual to discuss and elaborate on his lists. At this time the individual is also asked to identify an object he most likes in his favorite color.

Benefits—This activity enables participants to share aspects of themselves that others in the group may not know about. The game points out how much the participants know about each other and gives them a chance to get to know each other better. This is a fun game in which all can participate and have a chance to talk about themselves in an intimate manner.

B. THE MODERATELY HANDICAPPED-REGRESSED ELDER POPULATION

Elders who are moderately regressed are often confused about the boundaries between the past and present. At times, they are uncertain about where they are. Regression in this population can be caused by organic problems, social-emotional factors, physical illnesses, or a combination of variables.

Elders in this population may be clear in their thoughts, speech patterns, and actions, but have tendencies to drift in their sense of reality. When working with this population it is important to foster a sense of relationship, especially with the surrounding community or group, to prevent further confusion, withdrawal, and isolation.

It is also valuable for the therapist to note the influence of the elders' living situations on their physical conditions. This information enables the therapist to know the dimensions of the participants' illnesses and social conditions, and to understand the extent to which the two are interdependent. Knowing how the social setting can have a positive or negative effect on the physical, emotional, cognitive, and psychological health of elders can be very helpful in determining treatment plans and carrying out a vital daily activity schedule.

In creative arts therapy sessions it is important to stress the relationship of the elders' feelings and thoughts to their actions. A creative activity can help participants to see the creative product as a reflection of their feelings and thoughts. In this process individuals are reinforced in their sense of reality, self-esteem, and sense of being. The creative process and activity can play many roles and have many functions for this population.

Creative Arts Therapy Themes, Techniques, and Processes for the Moderately Handicapped-Regressed Elder Population

1. *The use of art and writing as therapeutic tools for improving reality orientation* (see chapter 3).
Benefits—This art and writing activity is a multifaceted orientation process which enables individuals to increase their awareness of their past, the present day, and possibilities for their future. Conscious and unconscious thoughts and feelings about participants' lives are uncovered and discussed through the art and writing experience.

2. *Theme-related art expression*—Have participants write about, draw, or paint symbolic or realistic pictures focusing on a theme chosen by the therapist or group. Themes related to family, friends, places, homes, and past and present experiences can be used to initiate the expression of feelings and thoughts about aspects of the participants' lives.
Benefits—This activity fosters reminiscence and reality orientation, and develops the participants' awareness of self, and feelings of self-esteem.

3. *Self-portrait*—Request that the participants draw or paint a self-portrait, using various art media, to express and explore their feelings about themselves. A recommended activity is to make life-sized portraits of the participants by having someone trace the outline of each participant on a large piece of paper tacked to a wall. Then have the participants draw and color in the details of their portraits, such as clothes, face, and jewelry.
Benefits—This activity helps participants recognize and relate to their self-image and self-concept, and enhance their awareness of their bodies.

4. *Written or oral journal*—Participants may use the journal format to record or speak about their daily feelings, thoughts, and memories. The journal can be written by participants, dictated to another for writing down, or spoken into a tape recorder. If written

journals are used, the participants can design and make covers for their journals.

Benefits—This activity helps elders to relate and keep a record of their feelings, thoughts, and life experiences. The journal reaffirms the participants' experiences at a time in their lives when it may be difficult for them to remember their past and to feel value in their present lives.

5. *Spontaneous drawing and painting*—This type of drawing and painting allows for creativity and fun without the restrictions and boundaries of many crafts. Also, it aids in the nonverbal communication of feelings and thoughts. The activity may be used to help participants develop the skills of drawing and painting. Several different types of art materials may be used.

Benefits—Drawing and painting facilitates the uncovering and free association of feelings and thoughts. It also helps participants to develop perception, eye-hand coordination, and spatial arrangement.

6. *Clay modeling and the use of molds*—In this activity, participants create free-form clay sculptures (abstract and realistic) to express feelings and thoughts, and to learn the skill of working with clay. Different themes (such as those from nature) can be a focus for clay modeling. When using clay molds, participants can easily create, paint, and decorate the objects they make.

Benefits—In clay modeling the fingers and hands are exercised (kinesthetic and tactile awareness) and eye-hand coordination is developed. Clay is a good medium to use because of the tactile sense of working with a pliable material. Participants learn to create an object and to complete a skilled task. Having a good-looking finished product from a clay mold or sculpture gives participants a feeling of achievement and self-worth.

7. *Collage*—Participants sort through a collection of pictures from magazines to create a collage. Have participants put together, design and glue, a collage around a theme. Participants can draw or write on their collage if they choose. Beads and other materials and textures should be available to add to their designs.

Benefits—Some of the benefits of making a collage are: reality orientation, reminiscence, group dialogue and interaction, and developing coordination by using scissors and gluing pictures on paper (use non-toxic glue and paper-cutting scissors). This activity can also function as a cognitive exercise in focusing participants on a specific topic or theme.

8. *Finger painting*—Participants use their fingers and colored

paints to create various forms and textures on paper. This activity focuses on tactile awareness and spontaneous, free form self-expression.

Benefits—Finger painting provides kinesthetic and tactile stimulation and expression of feelings, thoughts, and memories through a color and form picture; a fun activity.

9. *Music*—A process similar to that suggested for the minimally handicapped elder population may be used. With this population, playing songs for reminiscence and reality orientation is helpful. Also of use are musical exercises in which participants learn the melodies and words to songs and practice singing.

Benefits—This is a valuable group experience. Participants have the opportunity to relate and express with rhythm and beat, and to experiment with creating music. Also, as previously noted, this is an excellent exercise for reality orientation, reminiscence, deep and proper breathing, and other forms of learning.

10. *Movement*—Basically, the same process can be used as with the minimally handicapped elder population. However, most of the movements and exercises should be done sitting in chairs. Body movement is an important need for this population due to arthritic problems and lack of exercise. Massage techniques may be used for relaxing muscle tension.

Benefits—The movement (kinesthetic) process itself, exercising and stimulating the full body from head to toe, being in touch with the body and moving to music, can lead to a positive, joyful group experience.

The next activity is not primarily a creative arts therapy process, but is an activity which I have found to be useful in my work with the moderately handicapped-regressed elder population.

11. *Food activity*—Feel, smell, and discuss the topic of food; talk about restaurants that participants have gone to; discuss their favorite food and foods they like to cook; talk about their past experiences with cooking and possibly plan a meal for the future. The group session should also focus on the tactile and sensory experience of foods. Fresh food items for exhibition, cooking, and eating will enhance the activity.

Benefits—A few of the benefits of this activity are: tactile and sensory stimulation, reminiscence, reality orientation, and group interaction and discussion. This activity may also enable participants to learn about nutrition, and ways to shop for and prepare foods.

12. *Any of the other processes mentioned for the minimally handi-*

capped elder population may be effective if applied appropriately on the individual or group level.
Benefits—These activities may be of benefit according to the needs of the participants and the design of the activity or process.

C. THE SEVERELY HANDICAPPED-REGRESSED ELDER POPULATION

In the severely handicapped-regressed elder population, patients often have a confused awareness of their past, present, and the reality of their future. These patients are also, at times, confused about who and where they are. Patients with this condition often have a fixation on the past, possibly compounded by an anxiety about the present. This condition may be due to brain damage caused by strokes, debilitating illnesses, injuries, or severe social, physical, or emotional deprivations.

Because of this populations' limited ability to communicate verbally and limited cognitive abilities, awareness and learning are most accessible through the five senses. Important therapeutic tools and processes with this population are: reality orientation, sense and tactile stimulation, body awareness and feeling, verbal and nonverbal communication. The use of group interaction and group process fosters feelings of belonging among participants and displaces the dysfunctional egocentricity of the regressed elder. This experience helps participants to feel real boundaries and to have contact with others.

One of the major difficulties in working with regressed elders is in finding a way for the therapist and client to mutually communicate and interact. Through the creative arts therapy process, clients may relate feelings and thoughts in a spontaneous self-expressive manner using an art medium.

Creative Arts Therapy Themes, Techniques, and Processes for the Severely Handicapped-Regressed Population.

1. *The use of art and writing as therapeutic tools for improving reality orientation* (see chapter 3). This exercise can be adjusted to the needs and capabilities of the participants.
Benefits—The art and writing activity is a multifaceted orientation process which enables individuals to increase their awareness of

their past, the present day, and possibilities for their future. Conscious and unconscious thoughts and feelings about the participant's lives are uncovered and discussed through the art and writing experience.

2. *Clay sculpting and modeling*—Have participants make simple form sculptures using a non-toxic clay. The sculptures can be of nature, people, or objects. Another valuable clay activity, which can be done with the help of the group leader, is pouring clay molds. Participants can paint their clay pieces after they have been fired in the kiln.

Benefits—Some of the benefits of clay modeling are: tactile stimulation; eye-hand coordination; exercising the fingers, hands, and arms; self-esteem and personal satisfaction in creating an object.

3. *Drawing using a simple or common theme*—Participants can use felt-tip markers, crayons, or paints for drawings. The drawings should be based on a theme chosen by the group leader and/or the participants.

Benefits—The use of drawing to relate feelings and thoughts on a specific theme provides a focus for group discussion of particular topics. The process of drawing can also assist participants in developing eye-hand coordination and recognizing spatial relationships.

4. *Finger painting*—Participants use colored paints with their fingers and hands to create various colored forms as a focus for tactile stimulation, self-expression, and to evoke feelings and thoughts.

Benefits—This activity provides kinesthetic and tactile stimulation and a simple expression of feelings through color and form. It also is an easy way to make a picture and give participants a sense of their ability to create. The participants' actions are reflected on paper by the expressions of their hands. Bound emotional energy may be released through the free-form process of finger painting.

5. *Painting by brush*—A large selection of colored paints, a variety of brushes (especially brushes with large handles to make them easy to hold), and various sizes and colors of paper should be offered to participants.

Benefits—The free-form expression of color and form, through painting, provides visual stimulation, hand and arm exercise, and an opportunity to develop eye-hand coordination.

6. *Collage*—In this activity, participants create a collage around a theme using pictures from magazines. The participants should find the pictures they want to use, and then if needed the group leader can help to cut them out of the magazines. The participants should

design the placement of the pictures on the paper and glue the pictures down. The group leader may need to help the participants glue the pictures to the paper.

Benefits—The collage activity promotes reality orientation, reminiscence, cognition (i.e., picking out appropriate pictures for the theme of the collage), eye-hand coordination, and group dialogue and interaction.

7. *Music*—The group leader will direct the participants to sing songs and play musical instruments (rhythm band), focusing on simple songs and melodies. The songs can be those the participants are familiar with (evoking reminiscence) or new songs and melodies (as a learning experience).

Benefits—This is an excellent group activity which provides for fun, reminiscence, reality orientation, deep and proper breathing, and learning to be in touch with rhythm and beat.

8. *Movement*—Using background music, have an exercise/movement group while being seated. This activity focuses on body awareness, exercising the different parts of the body, and being able to recognize how the different parts of the body feel. Conduct exercises and body movements to music. Use touching and tapping body parts as a way for people to become in tune with their bodies.

Benefits—This activity enhances body awareness, improves circulation, reduces muscle tension, and provides an expression and acknowledgment of feelings through movement.

9. *Written or oral journal*—The group leader can use a tape recorder to record the participants' feelings, thoughts, activities, and memories or he can write them down. The participants may add to their journal through drawings, collages, paintings, poems, and simple writings.

Benefits—This activity enhances the participants' recognition of their feelings and thoughts about their daily lives and their pasts, and gives a greater significance and meaning to their lives as they reflect over their journals.

The following activity is not primarily a creative arts therapy process but is an activity which I have found to be important in my work with severely handicapped-regressed elders.

10. *Food activity*—Feel, smell, and discuss the topic of food: talk about restaurants that participants have gone to; discuss their favorite foods and foods they liked to cook. The group session should also focus on the tactile and sensory experience of foods. Fresh food items for exhibition, cooking, and eating will enhance this activity.

Benefits—Some of the benefits of the food activity are: tactile and sensory stimulation, reminiscence, reality orientation, group interaction and discussion. This activity may also enable participants to learn about nutrition and proper eating.

11. *Any of the other processes mentioned for the minimally or moderately handicapped elder population may be effective if applied appropriately on the individual or group level.*
Benefits—These activities may be of benefit according to the needs of the participants and the design of the activity or process.

An activity for all people: Listening, feeling, loving, laughing with, and sharing.
Benefits—The greatest gift to give is to share yourself and the greatest gift to receive is to have others share themselves with you.

The exercises, techniques, tools, and themes I have described for the minimally, moderately, and severely handicapped elder populations are a basic overview of activities which I have found useful in my work. These processes are generally applicable to many other groups or individuals of varying age, abilities, and handicaps. I have included only the basic design and steps in the activities. The skill and creativity of the therapist must facilitate and engage participants in the therapeutic process. The receptivity of participants to the particular modality, exercise, or activity is a major factor which needs to be taken into consideration in designing activities or a therapeutic program. In the experiential process of creative arts therapy there are many other valuable tools, techniques, and activities the therapist may discover as he develops a personal therapeutic style and process. I encourage the therapist to create, share, and discover together with the participant.

We are always only beginning.

GROUP PROCESS

The dynamics of group process in creative arts therapy sessions with elders can be very inspirational and therapeutic. The activity of elders working together reinforces a sense of community, sharing, and peer support. I design creative arts therapy sessions to be as comfortable and relaxed as possible, often with background music playing and refreshments nearby.

A group which I facilitated (sometimes with the help of nurses, orderlies, or volunteers) in a long-term care setting often consisted of five to twenty-five participants. This was sometimes a large group, especially for in-depth psychotherapeutic encounters; but, just the interaction of numerous people working and creating art together would often facilitate many personal breakthroughs. Members of the group inspired each other through relating, creating, touching sparks of compassion and humor, giving each other the acceptance to be themselves (even if it was to be withdrawn).

One of the valuable aspects of the group process was the individual discussions I had with participants within the group. These discussions aided the individual to be in touch with and at times work through a situation he was thinking of or a feeling he had. During creative arts therapy sessions I would walk around the table from patient to patient looking at their art work and offering participants an opportunity to verbalize their feelings and thoughts with me or with others in the group. These talks, involving one or more patients, were sometimes very intimate, occasionally explosive, and usually personal and meaningful.

In group and individual discussions, patients confronted many personal topics, such as family, friends, conflicts and good times, memories of their past, and of their lives in the hospital. The group process stimulated participants to encounter themselves and others in the group or clarified the ways they avoided personal and group involvement. In either case, participants could relate in a comfortable, intimate manner to myself and others.

When I talked with participants during an art therapy session, I usually attempted to bring to consciousness the participants' full situation and depth of personal feelings while giving them emotional support. I encouraged the participants to discuss the theme or idea of their picture or I pointed out an image for them to focus on and asked them to continue to express the deeper meaning of the picture. At that time, participants often chose to do another picture with a more specific feeling or theme in mind to explore further. When all group members finished their art expression (toward the end of the session), I would ask each person to share his feelings about the art experience and the group session.

Often in each session a particular mood or attitude would dominate the session. If a death recently occurred in the hospital, there would be a solemn or reserved mood. If it was around the time of a full moon, there often seemed to be a mood of quiet tension. I would look to the group dynamics for the interaction and discussion of issues and feelings. Living in the hospital was one major issue which all patients had feelings about. Group discussion on this issue often brought us closer together and deeply emotionally intertwined.

The creative arts therapy sessions were similar to a journey, with music playing in the background, some discussion by the therapist and participants on possible themes to explore, talk about the daily news, and a free hand to the art materials. We felt we were creating Noah's ark again, searching, coming back home to ourselves.

IN CONCLUSION

Metaphorically, the therapist must be the watchman in the forest for the traveler in the night: the traveler is the participant expressing his feelings and thoughts, coming to his sense of self. The therapist needs to guide the journeying client until the traveler finds his own light to brighten the path in the forest.

Relating, processing, and building a world from within helps the individual to develop an enriched sense of self, character, and stability as an individual. These components of self-integration are personally explored in a poem by three elders I have known.

Oceans

I remember the sea.
Seeing the whale,
being with my niece
and my husband.
I said to the lady that her flowers were pretty
as she handed them to my husband.
I remember the anchor,
the cold steel.
And then it started moving,
onward to New York.
We arrived there.
That's all I remember.
The water was blue.
I remember the storms.

Chapter 3

The Use of Art and Writing as Therapeutic Tools for Improving Reality Orientation

I. INTRODUCTION

In hospitals, long-term care settings, and community care programs patients may exhibit a loss of awareness, confusion, and disorientation. This may be due to physiological causes such as organic brain syndrome, possibly compounded by psychological causes such as depression and/or environmental conditions (lack of stimulus). In recent years the popular therapeutic treatment for disorientation has been "reality therapy," as developed by Taublee and Folsom (1966).

Reality therapy is based on repeating fundamental reality information accompanied by the use of props such as clocks, pictures, calendars, familiar household objects, and other items as visual aids. Testing and development of a form of this therapeutic technique was done at a long-term care facility with organic brain syndrome and brain dysfunction patients (Weiss, 1979). It was found that by augmenting reality orientation with an art and writing process and using themes to initiate discussions, participants exhibited an increased orientation to their previous problems, conflicts, and possible hopes for the future. Through this process participants discussed their current problems and feelings about the past and future.

II. REALITY THERAPY

Even though reality therapy programs have shown successful results in increased patient awareness of appearance and self-care, expression of more self-esteem, and increased compatibility in patient-staff relations, *reality therapy does have its limitations.* Since this form of therapy is basically a verbally oriented treatment, it is often not an appropriate or efficient modality for aphasic, regressed, nonverbal, brain dysfunction, or mentally ill patients. Reality therapy does not provide a stimulating, encompassing, learning experience but rather a passive form of rote memorization. This therapeutic technique may not provide individuals a chance to express their personal needs, demonstrate their abilities, or share their experiences. On the other hand, as Silver (1978) notes, the art experience incorporates and validates a person in his or her learning, emphasizing with nonverbal patients the content of the communication rather than the form, "subject matter rather than abstractions, demonstrations rather than talk." This suggests the importance of an active learning experience to allow for the maximum use and incorporation of information. Consequently, patients would benefit from a more participatory and multicommunicative mode of self-expression such as art, movement, or music therapy, as developed in the art and writing process with reality orientation.

III. ART AND WRITING TO AUGMENT REALITY THERAPY

The expressive art and writing process incorporates a person's interest and learning through self-expression and communication. This process offers individuals numerous possibilities and avenues of growth. By individual and group creative expressive experiences, interactions, and reality-oriented projects, the individual can affirm and expand his understanding. Hereby, the art and writing process facilitates increased stimulation and communication, therefore decreasing isolation.

IV. PROCESS

The art and writing reality therapy groups are approximately one hour long. Two or three sessions per week are recommended. During each session a different theme is chosen to be discussed and explored through an art or writing modality, whichever is preferred by the participants.

At the beginning of the session each participant is given a reality orientation questionnaire to fill out (see Figure 1). The questionnaire

```
┌─────────────────────────────────────────────────────┐
│             REALITY ORIENTATION FORM                  │
│                                                       │
│  NAME _____    DATE _____       │
│                                                       │
│  PLACE _____                          │
│                                                       │
│  WEATHER _____                          │
│                                                       │
│  TIME _____                          │
│                                                       │
│  TODAY I FEEL _____          │
│                                                       │
│  IF POSSIBLE I WOULD LIKE TO FEEL _____           │
│                                                       │
│  FOR LUNCH I ATE _____          │
└─────────────────────────────────────────────────────┘
```

FIGURE 1.

is designed to test the participants' grasp of basic reality information, and also aids as a learning instrument by repeating basic information and affirming it through the use of writing. When a participant is unable to write because of physical or cognitive limitations, the therapist fills in the answer blanks according to the participant's wishes. After the questionnaires are filled out, the group reviews and discusses the answers. The reality orientation questionnaire serves as a beginning impetus for discussion and other interactions in each session.

Following the questionnaire a theme is presented for discussion. A drawing, collage or written expression concerning the topic discussed is done by the participants. The art and/or written experience lasts approximately 15 minutes after which each participant displays and discusses his work with the group. This enables each participant to reaffirm the reality-based information concerning his life, and to share personal feelings and thoughts. It also allows for unconscious feelings and thoughts to be raised through the spontaneous art and writing experience. As the group discusses the pictures, the therapist reiterates the reality-based information each participant shares with the group, enabling everyone to learn from the speaker's experience. This process provides a checking system for the participants to react to and interact with ideas and concepts brought up by other participants.

V. THEMATIC CONTENT

Weekly themes are designed to focus on important areas of a person's life—living situation, friends, and interests. The first two sessions may focus on homes: past home or homes and present home or living situation. The second two sessions focus on friends and relationships: favorite friends and the most difficult acquaintances in one's life. The third two sessions focus on self-interests: favorite foods or gifts to receive or buy, and what one would like to give one's best friend or friends. The themes are selected because of their value as a stimulus and focal point for reminiscing, relating, and discussing.

Using themes to initiate discussion and facilitate the art and writing expression provides individuals with a more intimate context in which to express their sense of reality. It also allows for conscious and unconscious feelings and thoughts to be brought to the surface and discussed. The use of themes in sessions often facilitates the participants' reminiscing and understanding of their past in relation to the present. In a study at a San Francisco hospital art and writing reality therapy group (Weiss, 1979) it was found that in all discussions initiated by the use of a theme, participants often revealed and spoke about difficult and important issues of their past which still have an impact on their lives today.

VI. CONCLUSION

The use of a thematic art and writing exercise with a reality orientation approach helps individuals increase their awareness and remembrance of their past and present situation—for example, where they lived in the past and where they are currently living, people they knew and miss, their current acquaintances, feelings of conflict, pleasant times and hopes experienced in the past and present, and problems which still exist or influence their present life. In this process participants with major physical and emotional disabilities are given a variety of ways to express themselves, including drawing, writing, and collage.

The art experience helps individuals to focus on specific issues, with a supporting group discussion concerning each individual's thoughts and expression. As confirmed by Silver (1978), the art process enables participants, in a nonthreatening way, to realistically discuss and share important personal issues. The art process provides the individual time to sort out his thoughts while drawing, or the ability to immediately react on paper. This experience validates participant's feelings and ideas, enabling them to feel more confident and able to share intimate thoughts.

Reality therapy with an art and writing approach is not a matter of rote memorization, but is an incorporation and integration of reality based material. It enables the individual to use the information gained in the course of a lifetime. This process helps to develop self-esteem and integrity by allowing a person to learn, develop, and grow from his context in life, as opposed to the memorization of concepts of reality as in traditional reality therapy. The art and writing process is a multifaceted orientation process (past, present, and future) that brings together conscious and unconscious thoughts and feelings through the art and writing experience. This process gives clients a historic orientation to their life situation. By the use of the described art and writing techniques with a reality orientation group, participants show an increased orientation to their present situation and gain a perspective and understanding of their previous problems, conflicts, and possible hopes for the future (Weiss, 1979).

BIBLIOGRAPHY

Barnes, J. A. Effects of reality orientation classroom on memory loss, confusion and disorientation. *The Gerontologist,* 1974, *14*(2).

Birren, J. E. *Handbook of aging and the individual.* Chicago: The University of Chicago Press, 1959.

Brown, L. H., & Ritter, J. I. Reality therapy for geriatric psychiatric patients. *Perspective in Psychiatric Care,* 1972, *10.*

Busse, E. W., Aging and psychiatric disease of late life. In S. Arieti (Ed.), *American handbook of psychiatry.* New York: Basic Books, 1974.

Chafetz, M. Alcoholism and alcoholic psychosis. In A. Freedman (Ed.), *Comprehensive textbook of psychiatry.* Baltimore: Williams & Wilkins, 1967.

Citria, R. C., & Dixon, D. N. Reality orientation—A milieu therapy used in an institution for the aged. *The Gerontologist,* 1977, *17.*

Cohen, G. D. Comment: Organic brain syndrome. Reality orientation for critics of clinical intervention. *The Gerontologist,* 1978, *18*(3).

Crossen, C. Art therapy with geriatric patients: Problems of spontaneity. *American Journal of Art Therapy,* 1976, *15*(2).

Dodd, F. G. Art therapy with a brain-injured man. *American Journal of Art Therapy,* 1975, *14*(3).

Drewdney, I. An art therapy program for geriatric patients. *American Journal of Art Therapy*, 173, *12*(4).

Folsom, J. C. Reality orientation for the elderly mental patient. *Journal of Geriatric Psychiatry*, 1978, *1*(2).

Gubrium, J. F., & Ksander, M. On multiple realities and reality orientation. *The Gerontologist*, 1975, *15*(2).

Harris, C. S., & Ivory, P. An outcome evaluation of reality orientation therapy with geriatric patients in a state mental hospital. *The Gerontologist*, 1976, *16*.

Holderman, E. *Handbook of aging and the individual.* Sacramento: State of California Department of Health, 1975.

Miller, E. A management of dementia: A review of some possibilities. *British Journal of Social and Clinical Psychology*, 1977, *16*.

Rosin, A. J., Matz, E., & Shulmit, C. How painting can be used as a clinical tool. *Geriatrics*, January 1977.

Sandock, B. Organic brain syndromes. In A. Freedman (Ed.), *Comprehensive textbook of psychiatry.* Baltimore: Williams & Wilkins, 1967.

Silver, D. *Developing cognitive and creative skills.* Baltimore: University Park Press, 1978.

Taublee, L. R., Folsom, J. C. Reality orientation for geriatric patients. *Hospitals and Community Psychiatry*, 1966, *17*.

Vischer, A. L. *On growing old.* Boston: Houghton Mifflin, 1967.

Weinberg, J. Geriatric psychiatry. In A. Freedman (Ed.), *Comprehensive textbook of psychiatry.* Baltimore: Williams & Wilkins, 1967.

Weiss, J. C. *The use of art and writing as therapeutic tools for improving reality orientation for organic brain syndrome and brain dysfunction patients.* Unpublished masters thesis, Lone Mountain College, 1979.

Wershaw, H. J., Comment: Reality orientation for gerontologists. *The Gerontologist*, 1977, *17*(4).

Zeiger, B. L. Life review in art therapy with the aged. *American Journal of Art Therapy*, 1976, *15*.

Zwick, D. S. Photography as a tool toward increased awareness of the aging self. *Arts Psychotherapy*, 1978, *5*.

REALITY ORIENTATION: A CASE IN POINT

Mr. B. was a participant in the art and writing reality orientation group at a long-term care facility. He came twice a week for the scheduled eight weeks. Through participating in this group, he became more alert and gained an understanding of his past and present life.

In group sessions he began to discuss his long-term problem with alcohol. He talked about when his alcoholism started, the good times he had with the "boys," the difficulties being an alcoholic presented, and the effect it had on his health. Mr. B also discussed his home life in the past and the problems he had with women, beginning with his mother.

Mr. B became very fond of me, and I felt the same way toward him. We enjoyed each others' humor. He told me that when he was with me he felt it was an opportunity to discuss his feelings and thoughts about his present situation and his past, and through our interaction he felt recognized for who he was and what he was going through.

The week after the end of the series of art and writing reality orientation sessions, Mr. B had what the head nurse called a "slight stroke." He acted very confused; he did not know where he was, what day it was, or his name. Also, he did not know the names of other patients and staff. When I went to see him he recognized me and said how glad he was to see me, but he did not know my name nor what I did in the hospital. He acted as if we had a special relationship, and was very happy to talk with me, although he did not know what our special relationship was.

We had spent countless hours discussing his life, dealing with issues and problems, orientating him to his present life, and creating art work; but, the only thing he remembered was that we had a special relationship and he felt good when he saw me.

When I realized what had happened to Mr. B, and that he had forgotten about our talks and had become disoriented, I had many different feelings. I was upset that he had another stroke and seemed to be more "out of it" and confused, and I was a little bewildered by his feeling of a special relationship with me. After thinking about his situation, it occurred to me that in working with Mr. B, he had learned something he could not forget, which was not just of the intellect but of the heart. I felt that I had helped to give him an experience of himself that was so personal and meaningful, that in his remembering me, he remembered himself and his feelings in an unconditional, accepting manner.

* * *

Through my work as an expressive therapist in a long-term care setting, I came to understand that most people want to feel they are included in the process of life with everyone else; that their answers are found within their own heart.

When patients feel they are in need, they may think they want someone special to come and give them "presents" and take away their discomfort. However, I deeply believe they also want to be that special person and give "presents" of their love, their experiences and learning, and be able to receive love and understanding from others.

Chapter 4

Art Therapy with a Man
Who Has an Organic Mental Disorder
Due to Korsakoff's Disease:
Developing Self-Expression
and Self-Awareness

The term, Organic Mental Disorder, is a particular Organic Brain Syndrome in which the etiology is known or presumed. This disorder is associated with a dysfunction of the brain which may be temporary or permanent. The fundamental feature of an Organic Mental Disorder is an impairment of cognitive functioning with related emotional/behavioral disturbances. Korsakoff's disease, an Organic Mental Disorder, is due to a thiamine deficiency associated with prolonged use of alcohol.

Within this chapter I will describe the use of art therapy with a patient who suffered from Korsakoff's disease due to alcoholism. The patient, Jack, participated in the art therapy program for over twenty-one months. Through this therapeutic program, Jack began to experience physical, psychological, and emotional restoration and recuperation.

In 1975, Jack was admitted to a long-term care/rehabilitation hospital in a semi-comatose condition. He was in his fifties and had a long history of alcoholism. Although he partially recovered physically, after several weeks he continued to be confused and disoriented. He was soon diagnosed as having Korsakoff's disease. This syndrome is noted by impaired memory of recent events and by confabulation. James C. Coleman states, in *Abnormal Psychology and Modern Life*, that people suffering from Korsakoff's disease "tend to fill in gaps with reminiscences and fanciful tales that lead to un-connected and distorted associations.''[1] This was a very accurate ac-count of Jack's behavior.

Before his experience in the art therapy program, Jack rarely left his bedside, sitting in a wheelchair for a few hours each day. He did not walk, having lost this ability during his long recuperation. His joints were stiff and it was very difficult for him to bend his legs. He was a large person (about six feet tall, weighing approximately two-hundred-and-fifty pounds) and the orderlies did not have the man-power and time to give Jack sufficient exercise to help him regain his ability to walk. Consequently, he became a wheelchair patient. During conversation and activity Jack would often fixate on one ob-ject or idea. He spoke in a disoriented manner, often using the wrong words for what he meant to say and beginning many thoughts which he did not complete.

After participating in the art therapy program, Jack began to regain his physical, cognitive, and communicative faculties. He dis-played an improved sense of memory and thought comprehension, developed his ability to differentiate time and space factors, showed an increased awareness of reality, and was better able to express himself verbally and nonverbally. His ability to recognize and com-municate a range of feelings and thoughts improved considerably. Along with his development in self-expression, he exhibited an in-creased interest in reading newspapers and conversing with others.

THE ART THERAPY GROUP

I conducted an art therapy group twice a week for Jack's ward. Participants would sit in a closed circle around a table. This seating arrangement promoted a feeling of togetherness and interaction. Felt-tip markers, crayons, fingerpaints, acrylics, and an assortment of art materials and paper were placed on the table. The art materi-als were handed around from person to person so that everyone could choose from the materials without having to stretch.

In the beginning of each session, participants talked about their daily events, families, friends, and personal feelings. From these discussions, themes to focus the art expression usually arose. If no theme developed from the discussion I would introduce a topic or

---

[1]Coleman, J.C. *Abnormal Psychology and Modern Life.* Fifth edition. Illinois: Scott, Foresman and Company, 1976, page 420.

project for the group to discuss and explore. In some group sessions participants wanted to draw and paint spontaneously. At other times they wanted to express a specific feeling or thought in an art media.

When I worked with a group of participants who had major differences in their levels of cognitive awareness, I often offered each person a theme related to his or her situation as a focus for the art expression. The use of individualized themes enabled participants to acknowledge and express conscious and unconscious feelings and thoughts concerning a facet of their life, nonverbally through the art expression and verbally in the group setting.

When I first met Jack it was difficult to motivate him to join the art therapy group. He usually refused to leave his bedside or stop watching television. When I would ask him if he'd like to go to the art therapy group he normally said "No!" and held onto his bedrail in fear and defiance. After a couple of months of my requests he reluctantly began to join the art therapy group.

When Jack first joined the art therapy group he would randomly draw pictures and write stories about his life, regardless of the group theme or project. He seemed unable to concentrate long enough to draw on one theme. When he began drawing or writing he had a difficult time stopping and would often write or draw for over an hour during a session. While Jack was participating in the art therapy group he usually forgot about watching television or staying by his bedside and wanted to stay in the group as long as possible.

Jack enjoyed drawing and writing stories about his past and present life, but would rarely initiate any group discussion concerning his work. In each session, at the end of the art process, the participants would share and discuss their feelings, thoughts, expressions, and projects. Jack carefully listened to others but rarely took an interest in talking to the group. He would comment on his art work or writings only when someone asked him about it. However, when I looked at Jack's art work, he would share his feelings and thoughts with greater ease and spontaneity, describing the drawings and telling me stories from his life.

Jack often told his stories in a confused manner: the people, places, and times being interchanged at random. Usually his sense of imagination and reality appeared to merge. When he told his stories he seemed to be making them up as he went along, possibly confabulating the story line. Sometimes, while Jack wrote he would also draw scenes from the story on the same page. Most of his stories, drawings, and writings seemed to be a combination of the people and places he had known through his experiences as a merchant marine.

After a year of attending the art therapy group Jack began to tell me whether his stories were fact or fiction. This was a major milestone in his progress. As his ability to express himself developed he began to enjoy communicating and started to draw, write, and talk more about his life in the hospital.

Before Jack joined the art therapy group, the staff and patients never knew what Jack thought and felt. He was like a closed book, until he began to express himself in the group. He was thought of as a typical old sailor, filled with stories but quiet about his life. The more he came to the art therapy group, the more he seemed to recognize his own personal identity.

Through the art therapy process Jack began to develop new skills in communication, recall his past, orient himself to the present, and gain an understanding of his life. Jack's development of self-awareness and his increasing participation in art therapy and with others on the ward is elaborated within the following progress notes. These notes were taken from two years of observations of the weekly art therapy group in which Jack participated.

ART THERAPY PROGRESS NOTES

The diary of a man who was forgotten, confused, scared, lost within himself until he began to tell the story of his life.

August through September, 1977. I often asked Jack if he would like to be taken to the art therapy group (he sat in a wheelchair and needed some assistance). If he was watching television he usually refused to move, seeming almost hypnotized. I would try to divert his attention by some conversation, but he usually did not relate to or even seem to comprehend what I had said. He often replied, "I've been watching this show now leave me alone." Usually, when he watched television, if someone asked him to leave his bedside he would hold onto the bedrail or the nearest object, pleading not to go. He seemed fearful of any change and nontrusting of people in general. If by chance I engaged him in a conversation he might forget about the television and let me assist him to the art therapy group. When he finally came to the session he usually enjoyed it immensely, forgetting about the television and what he had been watching.

In the art therapy group Jack was very involved with his creative expression, almost to the level of an exclusive attention to his art project. He seldom spoke to members of the group but acted very interested when others spoke. He communicated freely with me when I addressed him about his art or writing expression. At the end of the art therapy session he usually exclaimed "I am not finished yet, wait a minute!" When I explained to him that he could take his picture or writing to his bedside to finish it, he would fold up his art work and stuff it under his wheelchair seat. Although Jack often carried his pictures and art materials to his bedside, he usually forgot about them unless a nurse or orderly reminded him. When reminded, he might work on his pictures unless the television was on or he had something else to do, such as to look at the newspaper.

Whenever I hung up Jack's art work he was very proud. If the hospital staff commented on his pictures or writings he would talk to them at length about his work. However, when a fellow patient commented on his pictures or writings he usually replied briefly. He seemed not to want to get involved in a long discussion as when talking with the staff. It was my opinion that Jack viewed the staff as his primary caretakers, and therefore took a much greater interest in communicating with them than with fellow patients.

In retrospect: Through the art and writing process, Jack had gained a valuable sense of communicating to others. For a man who rarely spoke this was a very important step. In the art therapy group sessions when I would ask him about his pictures he would tell me a story that often seemed like a fantasy, fragmented and without logical order. I felt his stories had touches of reality, but it was difficult to decipher what was true and what was imagination or wishful thinking. At times his train of thought would flutter between the present and the past, producing a conglomeration of ideas.

September 19, 1977. Jack was very involved in the art process today. The group was making collages by pasting different colors and shapes of tissue paper onto a larger sheet of paper. Jack worked independently on his art work, creating a collage and pasting down the pieces of tissue paper. He was quiet in the session and engrossed in the activity. I think he appreciated the physical activity of the task as opposed to sitting by his bed just watching television. At the end of the session he said that he was not finished with his picture and would want to work on it some other time. A few days later Jack told me he had completed his picture. I hung it up on the wall next to his bed. He enjoyed seeing his picture displayed and talked to the staff about his picture whenever they noticed it.

September 28, 1977. Today in the art therapy group session it took an unusually long time before Jack drew or wrote. He seemed to be pondering something. After forty-five minutes of thinking he began to paint a rainbow on the left-hand side of the paper (see Photo 4.1). He told me a story which went along with his picture, but I could not understand or follow the story because of his fragmented pattern of speech. He talked as if he was daydreaming.

October 3, 1977. The art project today was a group mural. Jack became very involved in drawing his story and talking with a group member. This was unusual for him. He rarely conversed with fellow patients in the art therapy group. On the group mural, Jack sectioned off boundaries, with a black felt-tip pen, for himself and for Mr. B who was sitting next to him. Mr. B had not asked Jack to draw a black border for his picture but he did not seem to mind Jack's action. He just acknowledged what Jack was doing. The drawing of boundaries by Jack seemed to be a nonverbal act of recognition and acknowledgment of Mr. B. It also may have been a symbolic act of protection for Mr. B.

Other members of the art therapy group did not seem to notice or comment on Jack's boundary lines in the group mural. One participant, who was severely regressed and confused, drew over his black boundary lines. Jack made no reply to this action. His boundary lines did not seem to serve the purpose of keeping other people out as much as it denoted an identity for himself. The boundaries seemed to be a confirmation of his private space within the group and, possibly, the hospital.

Jack said he drew a "pack horse on a mountain top" on the group mural and that his drawing had a "leg surprised excitement" which he did not explain (possibly he was referring to the feelings he had in his legs due to the extensive amount of time he sits in a wheelchair). Mr. B said he had the same feeling. Mr. B is a double leg amputee and often has discomfort and pain sitting in his wheelchair. This may have been the reason for his agreement about the feeling of a "leg surprised excitement."

It was interesting to see Jack and Mr. B relate to each other because they are two of the most alert people within the group. In the session, Jack spoke with Mr. B for a few minutes. Although they did not seem to be understanding the verbal comments they made to each other, they still enjoyed addressing one another. After this discussion Jack drew a line connecting his pack horse to Mr. B's picture. This was another nonverbal sign of friendship. The other

PHOTO 4.1. Jack's painting of a rainbow. September 28, 1977

group members, being more severely confused, did not even recognize or respond to the interaction between Jack and Mr. B.

October 5, 1977. The art project today was a group mural. Jack worked diligently on his drawing, not looking up from his paper to notice others in the group. He drew a picture of cars on a street at an intersection. He told me it was a picture of where he had lived. He explained his picture to me but the story was so fragmented and confusing that I could not understand it, nor make sense of what was going on in his picture.

Jack's drawings were becoming more complicated and sophisticated in line, style, and content. He commented that he felt good about today's picture and by the end of the session he said that it was completed. He made no further comment on the meaning of the picture. It was interesting to note that this was the first art therapy session in which Jack said that he completed his picture. This may possibly relate to his feeling better about expressing a past situation—having thought and felt about it enough to feel satisfied concerning this particular experience.

October 10, 1977. The group project was a mural. Today Jack did not speak to anyone in the group except myself. He drew quietly with great concentration. He first drew a moccasin and next to it a shoe and ankle (see Photo 4.2). He said that the picture was "a girl's shoe and ankle and a man's moccasin." The shoe and moccasin were facing in opposite directions. From our discussion and his drawing I came to the conclusion that he was symbolically representing the absence of female relationships in his life (as exemplified by the shoes facing in opposite directions). Jack had told me that he wished there were more females around. Since most of the nurses and orderlies are female I think he was referring to his desire for an intimate female relationship. As he spoke to me he scribbled on his drawing, adding to the picture, seemingly to reaffirm his words.

October 19, 1977. Today Jack drew a horse and said that the horse had "a nag in his neck." This picture was one of the most detailed drawings he had ever done. Jack still did not speak in the group unless he was spoken to. As usual, he was very engrossed in his drawing but would stop drawing to talk with me. In our conversation he said that he was confused about where he was. He spoke in a stream-of-consciousness manner, using various references to his past and present life.

October 24, 1977. Jack drew today with increasing detail and clarity of line. He drew the inside of a car, the steering wheel, and

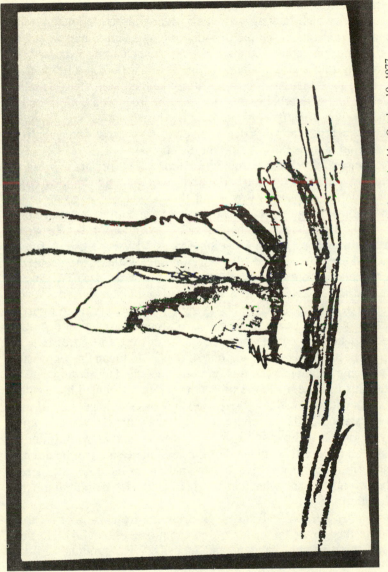

PHOTO 4.2. Jack's drawing of a man's moccasin and a woman's shoe and ankle. October 10, 1977

dashboard. In describing his picture he said "picks sick people up, a vehicle with a little horsepower, load two wheels." Mr. B, who was another participant of the group, said that Jack was talking about an ambulance, which Jack agreed. Jack never finished the picture. He told me a story about the picture that did not seem to have a beginning or end but rather sounded like his never-ending stories to be continually told and explained by Jack. For a person who doesn't talk a lot, Jack has much to write, draw, and explain. This quantity of verbal and nonverbal expression may be in compensation for his "quiet nature" or difficulty verbalizing his thoughts and feelings. Today's picture was very detailed, done with great hand control, showing an increase in his fine motor control.

November 2, 1977. The theme for today was free art expression using crayons, felt-tip markers, and colored pens. Jack wrote a story which he explained was about "Two stones, one going faster than the other. Figure out what the stones are comprised of because one is different than the other inside" (see Photo 4.3). He wrote more on his paper which I deciphered as "I wasn't use to figure some to keep preoccupied like working one of these, the problems where the stone out distance the rock of the same size. They were about the same size. Wish to hell the boys would get started. . .you get started." Jack seemed to be saying that he was trying to figure a problem out (the problem of the two stones moving at different speeds). I interpreted the sentence "I wasn't use to figure some to keep preoccupied like working one of these" to mean that he wasn't use to doing problems like this one but since he had nothing else to occupy his time he made the problem up. He concluded his written statement with the words "wish to hell the boys would get started. . . you get started" which I understood to mean that he wanted something to do, is waiting for something to do, and is getting angry about feeling bored. By the end of the session he said that he did not finish writing, but that he had an explanation for the different speeds of the two objects and what was inside of them. He didn't tell me the explanation.

November 18, 1977. Today Jack drew the front view of a cabin and described to me the inside of the cabin (see Photo 4.4). He said "it has three rooms, kitchen, and utensils." He continued to describe the inside of the cabin but I could not understand his description, nor decipher whether the cabin was something he had seen or been to, or was a figment of his imagination. From what I understood of his description of the house it seemed to be imaginary, but

PHOTO 4.3. Jack's writing. November 2, 1977. "Two stones, one going faster than the other. Figure out what the stones are comprised of because one is different than the other inside. I wasn't use to figure some to keep preoccupied like working one of these, the problems where the stone out distance the rock of the same size. They were about the same size. Wish to hell the boys would get started . . you get started."

PHOTO 4.4. Jack's drawing of a cabin. November 18, 1977

he could have been reminiscing about a place he had been. His ability to describe his pictures and express himself verbally as well as nonverbally through the art and writing medium has increased considerably. It is still difficult for me to figure out if his stories are real or of his imagination. In today's session he did not seem ready to talk about the reality of his stories. This may be due to our relationship still being in the beginning stages of building trust and exploring self-expression.

November 21, 1977. In the art therapy group Jack wrote on his paper "the levitian island between the berringer straight and the pacific ocean." He would not comment on his writing, but I had a feeling he was reminiscing about a place he had been. He did no drawing today but quietly pondered over his writings.

January–September, 1978. Jack has been participating weekly in the art therapy sessions. His art expression has slowly become clearer and the topics he discussed were more understandable. Some of the pictures he drew were: a man riding a horse (see Photo 4.5), horse pulling a wagon, and cars. He seemed to have a yearning for travel and to regret that he could not travel because he is in a wheelchair and rarely leaves the hospital. He often drew pictures of men fighting with guns and knives, or boxing. These pictures probably represented the people, places, and events he knew as a sailor and alcoholic. He drew pictures of cabins and huts which may represent the homes he once lived in, imaginary homes, or the home he is waiting to go to (see Photo 4.6).

In one art therapy session he drew a picture of a man and a woman in a field. After he drew this picture he talked to me about his romantic moments in the past. He would often write about women. For example, in one session he wrote on his paper, "Been wondering where the pretty and attractive girls are" (see Photo 4.7). As I previously mentioned, I do not feel Jack was just looking for pretty and attractive girls, but rather for an intimate relationship.

In retrospect: The nurses, orderlies, and social worker who worked with Jack had no idea of the personal history which he drew and wrote about, or of his feelings and thoughts of the present. Through his art expression and writings the staff began to learn more about Jack and relate to him on a deeper, more intimate level about certain issues and concerns. During this time he became more cooperative and wanted to join the art therapy group most of the time. This was a significant change from his previous behavior of refusing to leave his bedside to join any group activity. He has

PHOTO 4.5. Drawing of a man on a horse. Jan.–Sept., 1978

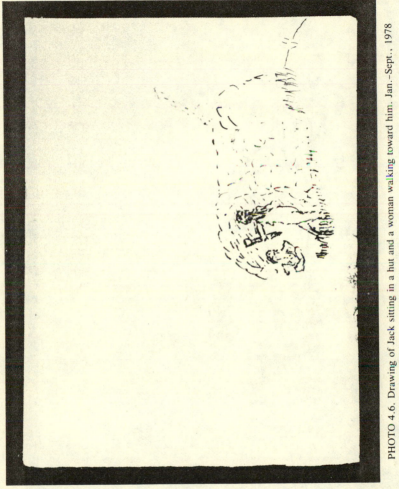

PHOTO 4.6. Drawing of Jack sitting in a hut and a woman walking toward him. Jan.–Sept., 1978

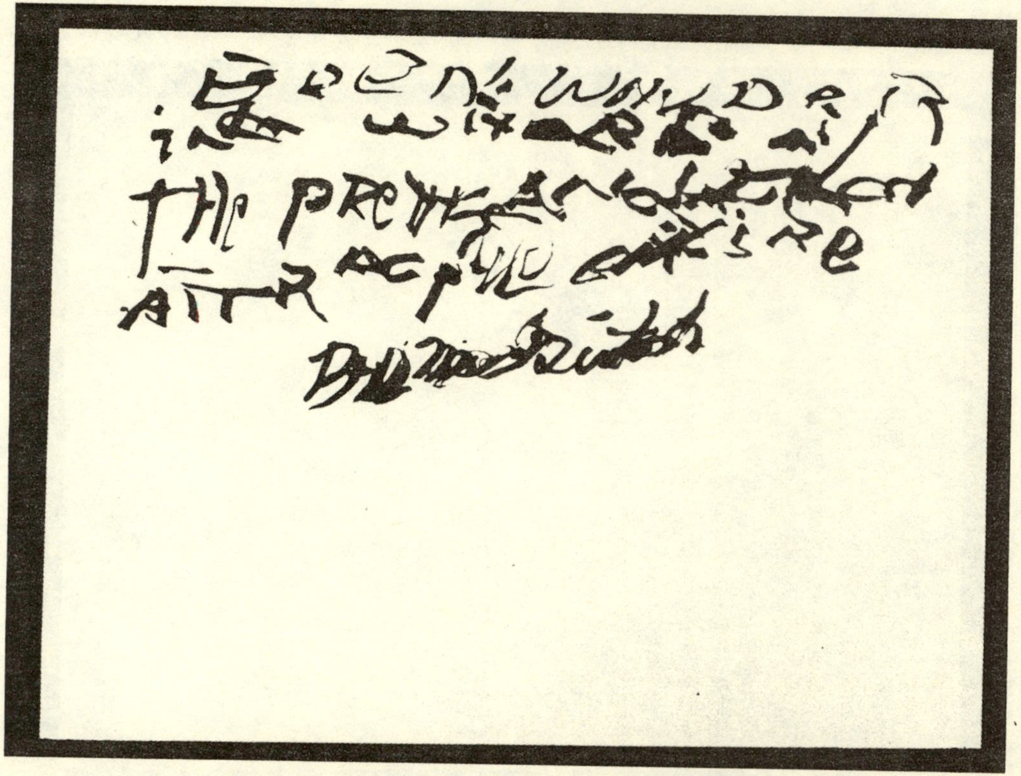

PHOTO 4.7. Jack's writing Jan.–Sept., 1978. "Been wondering where the pretty and attractive girls are."

become more expressive, understandable, and coherent in sharing his feelings and thoughts.

September 7, 1978. Jack wrote a poem today, but it was difficult for him to read aloud because of his poor penmanship. He was enthusiastic about his poem. I took some time with him to work on improving his penmanship. I suggested that he could practice writing and continue his self-expression in a blank book which would be his personal journal. Jack said he thought it was a good idea and would enjoy it.

September 21, 1978. I made Jack a large (fourteen by twenty-four inches) book which had ten blank pages for drawing and writing. Today he worked on the cover of the book, drawing a picture of the art therapy group (see Photo 4.8). In describing his drawings to me he said it was a fantasy picture. This was the first time he discerned to me the reality and unreality of his picture. I agreed with him that parts of the picture were not real, but I also pointed out the parts of the picture which he did copy accurately, particularly the table and art materials. He also drew two members of the group sitting around the table. I pointed out to him that there were other participants that he neglected to include in his drawing. He made no response.

September 28, 1978. Today Jack drew a picture on the second page of the booklet similar to the cover picture (see Photo 4.9). He drew people sitting around the art therapy table with art materials in the center. Jack wrote the date on the top of the page. His awareness of the date is aided by his recent daily reading of the newspaper. Jack told me in his Irish dialect that underneath the date he wrote "She's a cute little lassy and should be here before Shanghai sailing." In telling me this he sounded like a seaman waiting at the dock for his girlfriend before he ships off (this may have been one of his past experiences).

Jack then drew three people sitting around the art therapy table. He called these people "Bill, Chief, and Lucky." He told me they were his friends from Alaska. Throughout the session he made no other reference to these people, nor how they got into his picture of the art therapy group. As we were finishing up the session I asked Jack what he would like to call his picture. He said "friends of Alaska" and went back to his bedside with no further explanation. Jack's drawing and comments in this session are a good example of how he combined thoughts of his past with his present reality.

October 5, 1978. Jack titled his drawing today as "writing about the way things are." He wrote about his journey to a foreign land. It

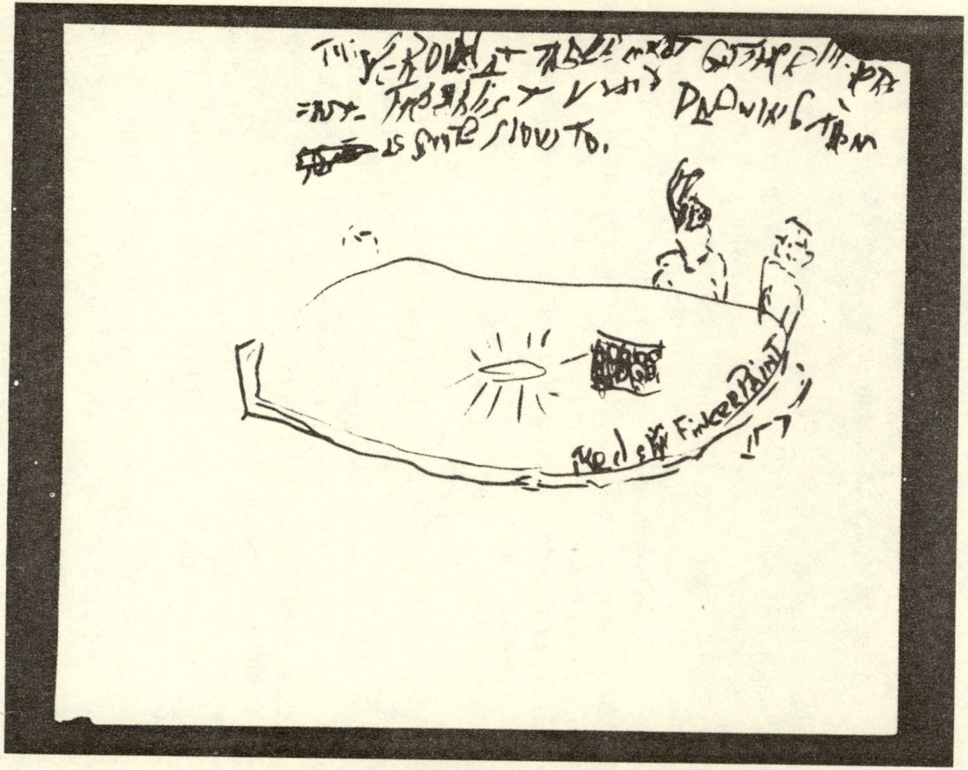

PHOTO 4.8. The cover of Jack's art and writing booklet. September 21, 1978. "Red skin fingerpaint."

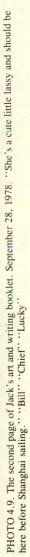

PHOTO 4.9. The second page of Jack's art and writing booklet. September 28, 1978. "She's a cute little lassy and should be here before Shanghai sailing." "Bill" "Chief" "Lucky"

was very difficult for him to read his writings because his words were written very close together in a script style. Underneath his writing he drew a large green cross on a mountaintop. This was a cross located near the hospital which he was able to see by looking through the window from his seat in the art therapy group. Above the picture he wrote ''The cross is facing on right in center of this page and soon a writing legable on the other page.'' Here he wrote and drew about what he was seeing and remarked about his penmanship. He is becoming more aware of his surroundings as noted by today's picture.

In retrospect: I feel Jack enjoys the art therapy group because he has a chance to communicate his feelings and thoughts verbally and nonverbally. While writing or drawing he can reminisce and ponder about his thoughts and feelings. Then, if he chooses, he can share them with others, sharing a part of himself.

Jack's communication difficulty and confusion may be due to both physical and psychological reasons, some of which are: Korsakoff's disease, the lack of intimate and meaningful relationships, and a feeling of displacement caused by living in a hospital with no place to call his own. For a person who has difficulty in sorting out his thoughts and sharing them with others, he has made great strides through the art therapy group. His relationship with the staff and fellow patients and his ability to verbalize has improved considerably and become more extensive. He now acknowledges who he is, where he is, and how he feels.

March 16, 1979. Today Jack did not want to draw but wrote a highly imaginative story that was difficult for him to read to me because his writing was almost illegible. The theme of the story had to do with finding a trail years ago. Jack would not comment on the significance or meaning of the story. This may have been to avoid dealing with feelings which came up from writing the story.

It seems that he is now aware enough to realize that the trail of his life has ended up living in a long-term care hospital. I do not think it is easy for Jack to accept the feeling of being ''helpless.'' From the confusion of when he was first brought into the hospital, to the awareness and recognition of where he is now, has been a long, and, at times, emotionally painful transition. With this awareness there may be anger, sorrow, and emotional pain. However, with time and by sorting out thoughts and feelings, Jack's acceptance of his situation may come, like a feeling of peace in his heart.

April, 1979. Jack was discovered outside the hospital wheeling himself down the road. He somehow escaped in his wheelchair from the third floor ward, went down the elevator, and out the hospital doors without being noticed. One of the nurses on his ward happened to be looking out the window and saw him traveling down the road in his wheelchair. The staff immediately went to get him. When he returned to the ward I heard he was upset and embarrassed. The next day I asked him about his trip out of the hospital. He said in a loud angry voice that he didn't want to discuss it.

Reflecting upon Jack's episode, I could not decipher if he was upset during and after the episode because he thought he could leave the hospital and when he was caught he was embarrassed about his confusion, or if he was upset because he didn't escape from the hospital and knew he had to live there. Either way he never mentioned the incident to fellow patients or staff on the ward. I also wondered if his acknowledgment of his situation, which he gained through art therapy, may have led to his decision to run away.

In retrospect: In the aftermath of the episode, Jack realized he was confined to the hospital. However, during the twenty-one months that I knew him I do not think he ever came to terms with this fact. His failure to deal with this issue may have been related to why he would fade in and out of reality at times. On a hospital ward it is easier for the patient to pretend that he or she is just there for a short while, avoiding close relationships, waiting to leave, rather than to deal with the issue of making the long-term care setting his permanent home. When I felt and understood Jack's situation, from my own perspective and experience, I could relate and empathize with him. For a man who has been around the world it probably got pretty boring living in a long-term care facility, in a ward of thirty patients, with no privacy and little chance for individuality or freedom to do what he wants.

After a patient lives in a hospital for a while he or she may become unattached to the outside world. The patient's whole world is in the ward, anything outside almost doesn't seem real. There is real security in hospital life: three meals a day, nurses and orderlies to watch over you, television entertainment most of the day (see Photo 4.10), and no fear of being cold. Patients give up a large part of their previous lives for these securities. Institutional living is not exactly a personal home, but many patients do not have a choice of where to live due to their disability and financial situation. As in Jack's case, he had no family, at least none that he was in contact with, and no one to take care of him or assist him. Life in the hospital was his home, a home that may take a long time for him to recognize.

PHOTO 4.10. Jack's writing and drawing. "T.V. gets better and better if could hook one up to a parking meter. Would not mind having another, ain't so much for me." "*Good Gosh.*"

ART THERAPY PROGRESS NOTES SUMMARY

I see no end to Jack's growth and development through his self-expression and communication, except in the limitations he sets by his own choice and those limitations caused by any organic damage he may have. In areas of cognition and communication, I do not feel that his organic damage is extremely severe. The large improvements he has made through his participation in art therapy proves the validity of rehabilitation in this case.

Jack's self-expression affirms his connection to his current and past life situation, lending him a firmer relationship with reality. He has achieved the feeling and experience of being able to communicate to himself and others. Jack has grown psychologically and socially from the increased awareness of his situation and has demonstrated an understanding of his life. Jack's progress is not comparable to a symptom reduction or a basic reality orientation, but is a personal transformation from a fearful, confused, fixated person to a reflective, thinking, questioning, communicative individual.

Due to the effects of chronic alcoholism, which resulted in an Organic Mental Disorder, Jack exhibited a lack of orientation, lack of judgment, poor memory, poor intellectual functioning, and the lack of ability to communicate his feelings and thoughts in a coherent manner. Through participating in an ongoing art therapy program for twenty-one months Jack has been able to slow down his cognitive deterioration and begin to develop his mental and emotional faculties. He has begun to recall and differentiate the past from the present, communicate feelings and thoughts more clearly, and share more of himself with others in verbal and nonverbal ways.

After his extended participation in art therapy Jack was not as fixated to the television. He was more willing to talk about himself or social events. For example, he developed an interest in reading the newspaper and commenting on the news. These changes in his behavior were due to the development of his relationship with me and others in addition to the meaningful, reflective expressions he created in the art therapy sessions. The development of trust between us, and his reduced anxiety about sharing his feelings and thoughts helped him to clarify his relationship to and outlook on life. Prior to his participation in the art therapy group, he would react to any change or disturbance by holding onto something nearby. Now, he is more verbal and expressive, and has increased self-control through developing confidence in himself and understanding his situation.

Since Jack has learned the ability to express his feelings and thoughts to a greater extent and orient himself to reality, he can now tell me if his stories are fact or fiction. In this way he differentiates between his imagination, reality, and wishful thinking. He now speaks to me about life in the hospital and a range of other topics regarding his past and present. Jack has not only made progress in self-expression through his experience in art therapy, but has also learned to communicate, share, and be in touch with his life (see Photo 4.11).

PHOTO 4.11. Portrays Jack reaching out to others through his writing and drawing. "Hi Fellows"

BIBLIOGRAPHY

The American Psychiatric Association. Diagnostic and Statistical Manual, III edition. Washington, D.C.: Author, 1980.

Coleman, J.C. *Abnormal Psychology and Modern Life.* Fifth edition. Illinois: Scott, Foresman and Company, 1976.

Chapter 5

Art Therapy with an Aphasic Patient: Relearning Communication Skills and Expressing Feelings

Mr. L, a forty-year-old black longshoreman, was striken with a CVA (cerebral vascular accident). The CVA left him with right hemiparesis (paralysis on the right side), possible dementia, and with aphasia. He was sent to a long-term care/rehabilitation hospital and placed on a ward for patients who need total care. He was one of the youngest patients on the ward.

Mr. L had been evaluated by the speech therapist to be aphasic and to demonstrate an apraxia of speech.* Stroke victims with right hemiparesis (left brain damage) such as Mr. L have a tendency toward language problems (e.g., aphasia, apraxia, perseveration). Mr. L usually appeared to be depressed, sleeping most of the day in his wheelchair or in bed. He acted withdrawn, generally silent, and when approached he stubbornly refused to interact with others or perform any task which was asked of him.

Two years after Mr. L arrived at the hospital I became the activity director and art therapist for his ward. Subsequently, I worked with Mr. L in group and individual activity and therapy sessions for two years. After the initial three months of encouragement and gradual participation in art therapy, Mr. L broke from his stubbornness, isolation, and withdrawal to participate in group activities and to communicate with his bedside neighbors. Through participating in art therapy Mr. L learned to communicate his feelings and thoughts, and became more outgoing and expressive. Mr. B was also able to establish a positive, trusting relationship with me. This

---

*The term aphasia refers to an impairment of acquired capacity to comprehend and use language symbols as a result of brain damage. An apraxia of speech refers to an impairment of voluntary speech movement.

chapter outlines Mr. L's therapeutic progress from being a person who was mute and withdrawn, to becoming a person who was able to interact with others, verbalize some words, and to increase his range and use of gestures and facial expressions.

MR. L'S BACKGROUND HISTORY IN THE HOSPITAL

During the many months of Mr. L's initial recovery from his CVA he refused to open his mouth. The staff told me that he had not said a word since his admission two years previously.

A year after his CVA, Mr. L went to the dentist. In order to examine his teeth, the staff had to pry open his mouth. They discovered that he wore dentures and that he had developed a mouth infection because his dentures had never been removed and cleaned. The infection had caused an edema of his mouth, lips, and cheeks. The dentist did not replace Mr. L's dentures. He feared that Mr. L would again refuse to open his mouth to have his dentures taken out and cleaned, and his mouth infection would recur.

The head nurse on Mr. L's ward commented to me that it was a mistake to not allow Mr. L to wear his dentures. She felt that since he did not have any teeth, Mr. L would feel more embarrassed and reluctant to open his mouth to talk and it would be more difficult for him to speak without his dentures.

The speech therapist evaluated Mr. L as having a poor prognosis because he would not respond to questions, was reluctant to open his mouth, and did not cooperate. I consulted with other staff members concerning Mr. L's lack of speech. Their theories included: guilt over something he said; guilt and sorrow over the ending of his relationship with his girlfriend (she stopped seeing him when he entered the hospital); a secret he was holding; depression over his condition and situation.

From my work with Mr. L, I felt there were other possible significant factors which limited his ability to communicate.

1. Fear of strangers: his unfamiliarity with the speech therapist might have made it uncomfortable for him to work with her, therefore he would refuse to respond.
2. Depression: due to the severe changes and limitations in his life, he was not motivated to interact with others or in activities, or to develop his abilities.

3. Embarrassment and difficulty in speaking: without his dentures and with an edema of the mouth and lips it was difficult for him to speak.
4. Physical impairment in his ability to speak.
5. An inability to comprehend the spoken word.
6. Mild dementia: due to his CVA, he possibly had some organic brain damage.

I felt that Mr. L's refusal to open his mouth and verbalize did not come solely from one cause, but that all six factors possibly played a part in his case.

Mr. L was a very difficult patient for the staff because of his physical and emotional problems. He rarely interacted with others and often seemed to be depressed. His blank facial expression made it hard to understand his nonverbal communication. The staff was uncertain of Mr. L's level of cognitive understanding and verbal comprehension. No psychological or intelligence tests had been given to him because of his refusal to communicate.

Mr. L looked like a man who had once been very handsome, but was now disfigured by an edema of the cheeks, mouth, and lips. He was an overweight, silent person who sat hunched over in his wheelchair, often with his head hung onto his chest and his eyes closed.

During the first two years Mr. L was in the long-term care/rehabilitation hospital he was tube fed. He did not open his mouth until one day he pointed to the coffee and doughnuts the nurse carried past him daily during breakfast. He first began to drink coffee, next he became attracted to the doughnuts. Eventually, he started to eat several types of food, and was gradually taken off tube feeding.

Around the time he started eating again, Mr. L began interacting with the nurses and orderlies on the ward. He would get their attention by shaking his head and arm, laughing and smiling, gesturing to the females to get a kiss or to imply that someone was sexy, or by making loud muttering sounds when he was angry. The staff liked his happy expressions, and gave him a lot of attention for this behavior. However, they treated him like a child, and did not foster or develop their relationship with him beyond a smile, a kiss, a playful joke, or a glance of nonverbal recognition. Even though the activity was good stimulation it was also a childish game that became habitual.[1]

The nonverbal communication between the staff and Mr. L was very important; the need for touching and recognition is vital. However, the lack of an adult relationship between the staff and Mr. L seemed to be detrimental to his therapeutic progress.

Mr. L would occasionally say a word when he was muttering in response to others. The prodding and jesting of the staff motivated Mr. L to laugh and interact. However, he fixated on a nonverbal level of communication for his primary and secondary needs (e.g., food, attention, social acceptance, extra concern by the staff). Mr. L communicated his needs through mutterings and nonverbal cues. He seemed to have little or no motivation to speak.

In Mr. L's situation, the staff used humor and jesting as a way to release tension and, possibly, to avoid their expression and acknowledgment of anger toward him due to his lack of cooperation, stubbornness, and refusal to participate in any activity. The use of humor and jesting by the staff as a major means of communicating with Mr. L did not give him the chance to have his concerns heard and felt in an adult way or to be addressed as an adult. Mr. L's behavior was either laughing and playing around in a childlike manner, or he was silent, withdrawn, and depressed.

I felt the preferred therapeutic approach with Mr. L was not to merely joke and "play" with him as with a child, but to give him a reason, a motivation to speak out and acknowledge who he was, how he felt, and what he thought. For a person suffering or rehabilitating from an accident, illness, or disability, the search and need for meaning and feeling in one's life is essential to the integrity and motivation of the individual.

There are many serious questions that need to be examined in order to understand Mr. L and his situation. How did Mr. L relate his feelings of anger, frustration, loneliness, and isolation without communicating beyond a laugh, a smile, or a handshake? What happened to his negative and troublesome feelings? What was it like for a man to be locked up inside by an experience that was so powerful or so devastating that he refused to open his mouth for two years? What does it mean to a man when there is no counseling, no psychotherapy, no aid in finding his sense of self-worth and identity beyond the contact with a nurse, orderly, or activity director? How does a man feel who has lost his profession, his social status, his home, his friends, his girlfriend?

When I first began working with Mr. L, in August of 1977, the speech therapist had put aside his case; the physical and occupational therapist claimed he had leveled in improvement; and the nurses and orderlies had him conditioned to a nonverbal pattern of responses. I saw Mr. L as still having potential to learn and grow, to engage in meaningful relationships and experiences, and to contribute to others. I wanted to provide a means for him to fulfill his potential.

Initially, Mr. L reluctantly joined the weekly art therapy group. This group had five to ten participants from his ward. In these sessions I usually asked the participants to choose the color of paper they wanted to work with and then taped the paper down so that it would be easier for them to draw. (This was especially helpful for those patients who could not both draw and hold the paper in place because they only had the use of one arm. With those patients who had the use of both arms, I often would not tape their paper down so they could adjust the paper to their creative needs.) Next, I would offer the participants a selection of crayons, felt-tip markers, and pastels. Normally, I had background music playing during the session.

The art therapy group focused on spontaneous drawing, painting, and clay work. With certain patients I would suggest a theme on which they could focus their art expression. But, because of Mr. L's defensiveness and fear of unfamiliar situations, at first I encouraged him to draw anything he wanted in a spontaneous free style. This helped to reduce his inhibitions and to foster communication.

In future art therapy groups I would use a withholding technique to see if he could react and communicate his feelings. Mr. L seemed to cut himself off from communicating his thoughts with others. He tended to express himself in a playful or a withdrawn manner void of a mature, sincere feeling-level response. The withholding technique I used would momentarily frustrate him, creating some anxiety and stress in his activity, motivating him to express his feelings and thoughts. This technique was also used to counteract his withdrawn and regressive behavior (such as sleeping in his wheelchair during an activity, and not interacting with others). During moments when he was annoyed, he would mutter loudly and angrily, sometimes for ten minutes. At those times he communicated his feelings and thoughts strongly. I came to feel that Mr. L could talk, given the appropriate opportunities and handling of his situation. Through Mr. L's participation in art therapy, he eventually was able to relate to his art work and to others in a spontaneous self-directed manner.

The following progress notes were taken from my observations of the weekly art therapy group in which Mr. L participated for two years.

ART THERAPY PROGRESS NOTES

August through September, 1977. In the first few art therapy sessions Mr. L did not care to draw, but just sat watching the others. In these sessions he always enjoyed the music and responded by shaking his head, snapping his fingers, and at times, tapping his foot. When he finally did draw he usually grabbed one crayon and drew small circles (see Photo 5.1) in an ordered, perseverated manner (perseveration is the continuation of a behavior or action after the activity has occurred when the stimulus is no longer present[2]). Mr. L's perseverated style of drawing may be an example of a repetition that fills a void in his activities. After drawing he usually slowly closed his eyes and gradually fell asleep.

In the first few art therapy sessions I had to coax him to draw. He acted as through drawing was a very childish activity in which he did not want to get involved. For a longshoreman with his background, this perception was probably correct.

In later sessions, the art therapy group worked on group murals. Mr. L usually drew in a very confined area in front of himself, not exploring any other areas on the paper (see Photo 5.2). When he completed a picture, I would always ask him about it. He'd often reply by hitting the picture with his hand as if to declare "This is mine!" Other times, he would get angry and yell incoherent syllables. He seemed to be saying "This is what I have done. Now, leave me alone!" To have Mr. L respond verbally, even though he was incoherent in his anger and frustration, was an accomplishment.

After the first few sessions, Mr. L was more alert while participating in art therapy. Also, he and I developed an affinity for each other. Mr. L liked my jokes, responding by laughing, smiling, and muttering sounds. I liked his spontaneous enthusiasm, especially since most of the patients on his ward were regressed and nonverbal.

September 28, 1977. During today's group Mr. L sat immobile in front of his art materials for fifteen minutes. He did not respond until a familiar female social worker entered the room. He immediately got excited, greeting her and shaking her hand. She painted his name on the paper which was in front of him. He then scribbled over the whole page in pencil and dabbled paint on it. (These scribbles were the beginning of what I have defined to be his stylized handwriting because it looks like script handwriting; see Photo 5.3). This was the first time he covered the full page with his writing.

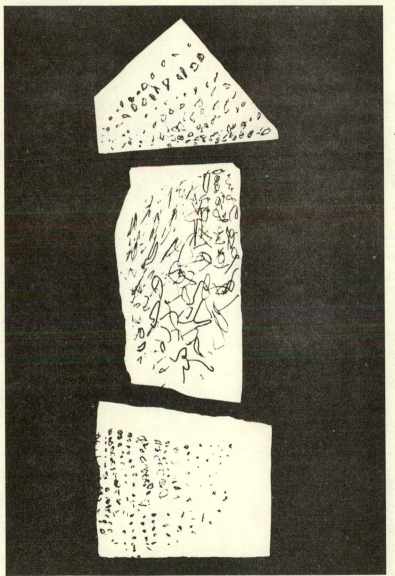

PHOTO 5.1.—Examples of Mr. L's drawings done on three group murals.

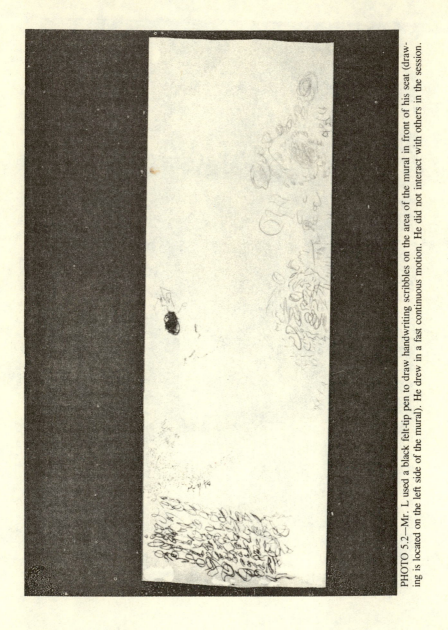

PHOTO 5.2—Mr. L used a black felt-tip pen to draw handwriting scribbles on the area of the mural in front of his seat (drawing is located on the left side of the mural). He drew in a fast continuous motion. He did not interact with others in the session.

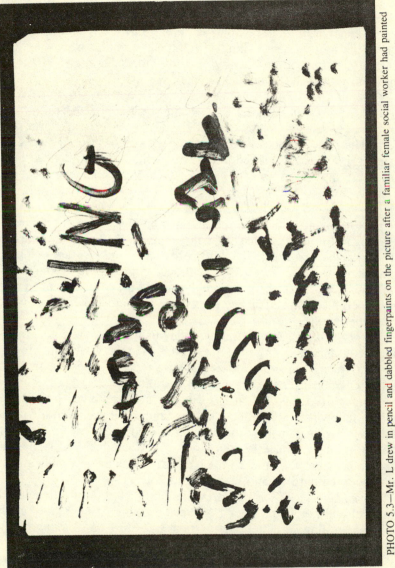

PHOTO 5.3.—Mr. L drew in pencil and dabbled fingerpaints on the picture after a familiar female social worker had painted his name on the paper. September 28. 1977

October 4, 1977. Mr. L was feeling very good today, responding to the music by snapping his fingers. Without any verbal directions or encouragement, he picked up a crayon and covered his sheet of green paper with long, continuous oblong scribbles (another example of his stylized handwriting). I felt these scribbles were a written communication to himself, myself, and others he knew. When he finished writing he smiled and looked very satisfied.

October 10, 1977. The patients in the art therapy group decided to make a group mural. Mr. L drew in a small confined area in front of him. He seemed depressed and drew small circles in a neat pattern. His drawing looked like he was perseverating (see Photo 5.1, page 85). When he finished the drawing, he lowered his head onto his chest and closed his eyes as if to signal his withdrawal from the activity and group.

October 17, 1977. Today, Mr. L was happy, drawing and moving his head and arm to the music, snapping his fingers to the beat. He began to mutter sounds of enjoyment in rhythm to the music. This was the first time I saw him verbalizing in a pleasant manner, devoid of any childish behavior, without any prompting from myself or others. Mr. L acted very friendly toward me. I have noticed that his mood picks up and he becomes more animated whenever I walk onto the ward.

October 24, 1977. Mr. L drew today using only one color, making a configuration with long lines. I defined this type of drawing to be his "picture-drawing" style because the lines seem to make a representational picture.

Today Mr. L had his first truly enjoyable, involved interaction with a fellow patient. A rubber ball had fallen between himself and a fellow wheelchair patient and they struggled to pick it up for over fifteen minutes until they succeeded. They laughed and smiled at each other after they picked the ball up. It was an accomplishment they worked hard on and looked proud of.

November 2, 1977. Mr. L drew his first picture in which he used vertical and horizontal lines ("picture-drawing" lines) along with his handwriting scribble. The vertical lines looked as though they represented a tree and the horizontal lines seemed to represent a sky. On the left side of the picture between these lines were his script handwriting scribbles. This was the first picture Mr. L drew using two styles of drawing (see Photo 5.4).

November 8, 1977. Mr. L began to draw with unusual speed, making noises with his crayons, and forming circles and dashes. This was his attempt to further explore sounds and visual images. I

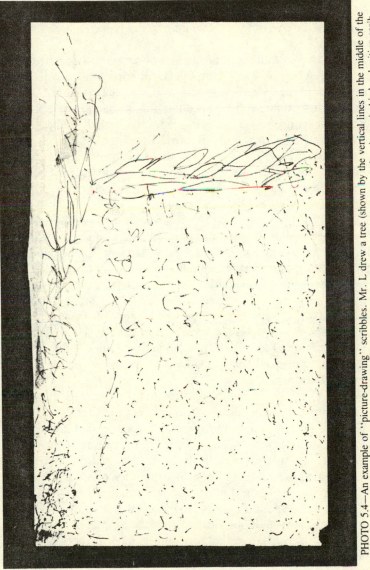

PHOTO 5.4—An example of "picture-drawing" scribbles. Mr. L drew a tree (shown by the vertical lines in the middle of the page), the sky (represented by the horizontal lines at the top of the picture), and wrote on the picture in his handwriting scribble. November 2, 1977

have defined this style of drawing to be his visual and auditory experimentation (see Photos 5.5 and 5.6).

November 18, 1977. Mr. L covered three-fourths of his paper with stylized handwriting lines while making tapping noises with his crayon.

The head nurse told me that Mr. L spoke a word to her this past week. She felt that he was trying to ask for something. I was feeling more confident that Mr. L was able to talk, but I could not pinpoint his limitations or name the particular major barrier in his speech problem—hearing, speaking, language, dementia, depression, a withdrawn attitude, or a combination of problems?

November 23, 1977. Today, for the first time Mr. L carefully picked out his crayon instead of choosing randomly as he usually did. His drawing was erratic and free style. As before, he continued to make noises with his pen and crayon.

At the end of the session I gave him a toy piano to play with. Mr. L played the toy piano for over ten minutes, exhibiting good concentration. Then I asked him, off-handedly, how he liked living in the hospital. He responded by shaking his head and motioned that he did not like living there. I asked him if he wanted to leave, he shook his head yes. I told him that he needed to learn to talk and communicate better. He shook his head to motion that he agreed. I asked him if he would like to go to speech therapy to learn to talk. He motioned his head yes and agreed to go. I informed the head nurse of our talk and his decision, and asked her to make an appointment for Mr. L to see the speech therapist.

November 30, 1977. The head nurse told me that Mr. L went to speech therapy, but would not cooperate with the therapist. I am not certain why he refused to participate in speech therapy. It might have to do with a fear of or an uncomfortable feeling with strangers (he did not personally know the speech therapist), fear of a new situation, or embarrassment about his inability to speak clearly.

When I reflected upon this situation, I thought that Mr. L might have learned to respond to the nurses, orderlies, and myself (people he saw a lot of) through our gestures and the tone of our voice. This is a common nonverbal communication pattern for people who are aphasic.[3] If true of Mr. L, I could understand why he would have considerable difficulty understanding strangers.

Later that day I asked Mr. L why he did not cooperate with the speech therapist. He did not respond to my question. I then told him that he probably would not be discharged from the hospital until he

PHOTO 5.5—An example of Mr. L's visual and auditory experimentation style of drawing. November 8, 1977

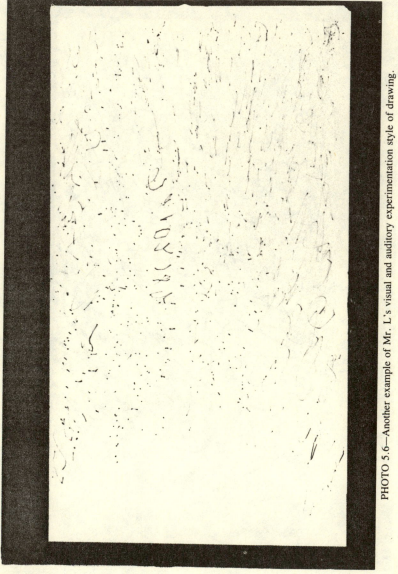

PHOTO 5.6—Another example of Mr. L's visual and auditory experimentation style of drawing.

learned to communicate better. I explained that he needed to communicate to be able to meet his needs. He would not respond to this statement either. I felt he was avoiding what I was saying. It occurred to me that for him to learn to talk might feel like an overwhelming task. Possibly, he would rather avoid learning to talk, than try to cope with the stress of learning and the possibility of failure.

January and February, 1978. Mr. L went into a state of depression and withdrawal from others (isolating and sleeping often). This may have resulted from being without his family during the Christmas season. Within these two months he rarely joined the art therapy sessions, and he seldom participated with me in individual activities.

March 2, 1978. Mr. L has begun to come more often to the art therapy group sessions. Today, he carefully picked out his crayons, and covered three-fourths of a large sheet of paper with his handwriting scribbles (see Photo 5.7). He was tapping his foot and nodding his head to the music, really enjoying the session.

March 9, 1978. Mr. L drew with a tighter style of handwriting scribbles and changed to a different colored crayon when he began to draw on a second sheet of paper. This was the first time he changed colors for the second drawing, possibly signifying the importance of the picture and/or a change in his feeling while drawing. His drawing style was becoming more spontaneous, he seemed to have more energy when he was drawing, and he was more enthusiastic about it. He now drew primarily in his handwriting scribble style.

April 6, 1978. Mr. L and I drew together on one sheet of paper using different colored pens and crayons (see Photo 5.8). At first he was apprehensive, but then paralleled my writing of words with his handwriting style of scribbling words. When I drew a picture he paralleled this with his "picture-drawing" style. We drew together for about fifteen minutes and then I had to leave. While I was gone he drew four more pictures with different colored crayons. This showed his enthusiasm, self-motivation, and enjoyment in communicating through the art and writing medium.

ART THERAPY PROGRESS NOTES SUMMARY

Mr. L has taken his first steps in relearning to communicate. By developing a repertoire of nonverbal and verbal means of expressing himself (e.g., through drawing, painting, facial gestures, mumblings, and verbalizations) he can communicate a variety of thoughts, feelings, and experiences. I feel it is now important to find

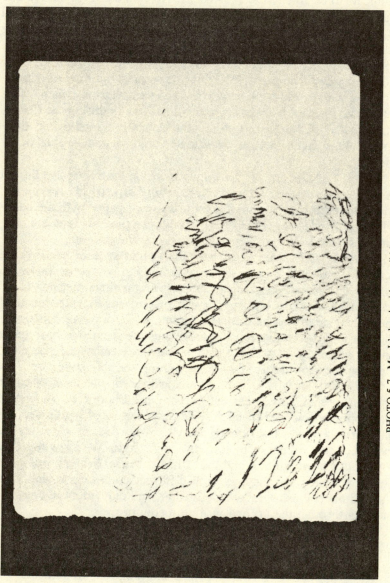

PHOTO 5.7—Mr. L's handwriting scribbles. March 2, 1978

94

PHOTO 5.8—This picture was done by Mr. L and the art therapist, working together, paralleling drawing and writing. April 6, 1978

out the extent of his abilities and the mode through which he can best communicate.

I have focused my work with Mr. L on meeting him at the model of his world, using a non-threatening mode for self-expression to avoid his defense mechanism of withdrawal. I also designed my therapeutic approach to engage him at his level of communication in an adult manner without reinforcing his tendency to develop a childish relationship to the activity or interaction. His world, like that of many aphasic people, can be very threatening.

> The aphasic patient needs strong defenses. Like anyone who, suddenly in the midst of the journey of his life has found himself alone in a dark woods where the straightway is lost, the aphasic patient knows despair.[4]

When I first met and talked with Mr. L he would not reply. He only looked at me and smiled. After six months of working together in activities and art therapy, he began to answer me through forceful mumbling sounds. Through the dynamics of our relationship he broke from his fear of communicating. I saw this development between us manifesting in his interactions with others. Now, after two years of participating in art therapy, Mr. L needs to develop appropriate verbal and nonverbal skills to enhance his communication with others. Through our work together in art and recreational therapy and from our intimate exchanges, Mr. L and I developed a solidarity in our relationship. The confidence and familiarity in expressing himself, which Mr. L experienced through our relationship and in his participation in art therapy, gave him the freedom for further personal development.

The following tables chart the behavioral changes, growth, and learning facilitated by the art therapy process.

TABLE 1: Previous Behavior vs. New Accomplishments in Art Therapy

Previous Behavior (initial participation)	New Accomplishments (after 1½ years of participation)
1. ashamed of art work	1. proud of art work
2. contained and extremely rigid drawing style	2. varied and contrasting drawing style

Table 1 (continued)

3. drawing in a small, limited area	3. drawing covers the whole page or several parts of the page
4. does not care what color he uses	4. picks colors selectively and carefully
5. uses only one color	5. uses different colors
6. draws only by himself	6. draws with others
7. does not follow or respond to others in drawing	7. can follow someone else in drawing and responds to others in drawing

TABLE 2: Cognitive and Emotional Changes

1. He now experiments in drawing and in making sounds.
2. He seems more relaxed in expressing himself.
3. He has learned new verbal and nonverbal skills in communicating.
4. He shows an increased ability to express himself in various modes—visual, sensory, and aural.
5. He exhibits an increased integrity and pride in his art work as shown by his verbal and nonverbal comments. He is now more territorial about his art work and enjoys showing off his pictures.
6. He seems to have gained a positive feeling and confidence that he can communicate and someone will listen and understand him.
7. He has been able to express himself and communicate with others, most noticeably through his relationships with the staff and patients.
8. He has made a friend—a trusting relationship with the art therapist.

TABLE 3: Motor and Visual Skills Learned through Participating in the Art Therapy Process

1. appropriate manipulation of objects (art tools and materials)
2. color selectivity
3. correct directional movement of paper for adjustment in drawing

Table 3 (continued)

4. increased perception and ability to work with various colors, forms, and sizes of materials
5. increased ability to adapt different materials for self-expression
6. able to copy another person's actions
7. able to participate with another person in an activity

CONCLUSION

Mr. L's development of self-expression with the assistance of art therapy intervention proved very successful, as noted by his changes in behavior, communication, and verbal and nonverbal expressions (see Tables 1, 2, and 3). At first Mr. L was a very difficult patient because of his initial stubbornness and depressed manner, and the staff's lack of knowledge of his capabilities and limitations. At times, I could only interpret how I thought he felt and what he was thinking. Initially, I had no idea about Mr. L's view of the world, but, he slowly shared his world with me by expressing himself through his eyes, his laughter, his forceful and agitated handshake, and through his art work and writings.

If he felt defiant, he drew hard and fast. If he felt angry, he would mumble loudly and almost rip the page with his crayon. When he was depressed, he would draw circles in a perseverated manner in a confined area of the paper. When he felt good and happy, he would often scribble in his handwriting style or create a picture in his "picture-drawing" style.

Through my work with Mr. L, I came to understand that each person has a particular way of approaching the world and a distinct view of the world. If I push a man to explore his world, to show it to others, he may defend himself and withdraw. If I encourage a person and acknowledge his struggles, he may respond. If I accept a man and sit with him, relating to his world, he will often share it with me.

After two years of participating in art therapy, Mr. L began to express himself, relate feelings and thoughts, and share with others. These actions demonstrated that he had overcome his first major hurdle—learning new ways to relate and communicate. However, Mr. L will manifest the real extent of his progress as he pursues relationships, acknowledges and communicates his feelings and thoughts to himself and others, and through the opportunities provided to him in the context of his setting.

Drawing Styles Of Mr. L

1. Perseverated Circles

An example of this type of drawing is in Photo 5.1, page 85.

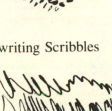

2. Handwriting Scribbles

An example of this type of writing is in Photo 5.7, page 94.

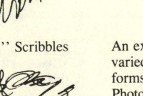

3. "Picture-Drawing" Scribbles

An example of Mr. L's varied line drawing which forms a picture is in Photo 5.4, page 89.

4. Visual and Auditory
   Experimenting

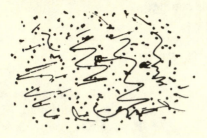

An example of Mr. L's experimentation with tapping sounds and various drawing techniques is in Photo 5.5, page 91.

NOTES

1. Schuell, H., and Jenkins, J. J., and Jimenez-Pabon, E. *Aphasia and Adults.* New York: Harper and Row, 1964, page 318.
2. Travis, L. E., ed. *Handbook of Speech Pathology and Audiology.* New York: Meredith Corp., 1957, chapter 50.
3. Schuell, H., Jenkins, J. J., and Jimenez-Pabon, E. op. cit. page 318.
4. Travis, L. E., ed., op. cit. chapter 50.

BIBLIOGRAPHY

"Disorders of Communication." Proceedings of the Association for Research in Nervous and Mental Disorders: Dec. 7-8, 1962. New York: Hafner Publishing Co., 1969.

Fowler, R. S. and Fordyce, W. E., *Stroke: Why Do They Behave That Way?* Washington State Heart Association, 1974.

Goldstein, K. *Language and Language Disturbances.* New York: Grune and Stratton, 1948.

Russell, R. and Espir, M. L. E. *Traumatic Aphasia.* New Jersey: Oxford University Press, 1961.

Schuell, H. and Jenkins, J. J., and Jimemez-Pabon, E. *Aphasia and Adults.* New York: Harper and Row, 1964.

Siev, E. and Freishtat, B. *Perceptual Dysfunction in the Adult Stroke Patient: A Manual for Evaluation and Treatment.* Thorofare, New Jersey: Charles B. Slack, Inc., 1976.

"Stroke, A Guide For The Family." New York: American Heart Association, 1969.

Travis, L. E., ed. *Handbook of Speech Pathology and Audiology.* New York: Meredith Corp., 1957.

Wepman, J. M. *Aphasia in the Family.* New York: American Heart Association, 1969.

Chapter 6

Dying, A Meaningful Experience: Encountering the Process Through Art Therapy

PART ONE: DYING, A CULTURAL DENIAL

In our society dying is generally seen as the sad conclusion to existence, rather than as a sacred part of life. This attitude creates a fear of death. The fear is not limited to the patient, but is shared by family and friends involved. The therapeutic modality of art therapy can help facilitate an acceptance and understanding of the dying process and aid the patient and family in dealing with their fears.

The social isolation in institutions and hospitals can reinforce a tendency of the dying patient to regress and withdraw.[1] Institutions often do not administer sufficiently to the psychological process of the dying patient, but focus on the physical needs. Many hospitals do not offer counseling for the dying person and his family. Instead, they pacify the patient and the bereaved. Denial by the family, the dying person, friends, or involved staff of the psycho-social dynamics of the dying process can result in guilt, passive acceptance, and refusal to experience and deal with the reality of the situation.

At times families avoid experiencing the loss of their loved ones. They abandon their feelings and deny the natural process of grieving. The act of holding back an overwhelming emotional experience is later compounded by the guilt of never having grieved. A common ritual practiced by the family and friends of the dying person is to assume a facade of acceptance or resignation. This acceptance is often a passive withdrawal from the reality of death. Dying with dignity is not a passive acceptance of death or a mere resignation to the fact of death, but requires an emotional sharing by the patient, family members, and involved individuals.

---

[1]Theodore Sardine, *Studies in Behavioral Pathology.* New York: Holt, Rinehart, and Winston, 1962.

The fear of death in our society, the denial of families, the blind treatment in institutions—all compound the patient's regression. A dying person often suffers an emotional and spiritual death when he experiences a loss of self-esteem and identity. The patient withdraws, becoming socially and culturally isolated and noncommunicative. This culminates in the patient's mental, physical, and emotional deterioration, binding the patient's spirit and making a child out of an adult.

PART TWO: DEATH AT MY DOORSTEP

On May 5, 1972 I experienced a near-death state. Due to a car accident I lapsed into a coma which lasted fourteen days. A six-month intensive recuperative process followed my awakening from the coma. During this time I felt the emotional turmoil and magnitude of the dying process and its social implications.

After I regained consciousness, people would ask me how I was. Most of the time I replied automatically (without thinking), "Fine, life is beautiful." I had no pain, no feeling in my body. Instead, I had an intuitive sense of being a part of everything and a sense of knowing without a doubt that life is beautiful and perfect.

My experience in the hospital did not fit into others' concepts of my situation. I spoke slowly and repetitively. People acted as though I was delirious, or they treated me like a child. They could not relate to me as an individual who felt great about just being alive. Instead, they focused on how "lucky" I was to have lived through the accident and on the numerous possibilities of my being mentally and physically disabled. Even though I could not communicate my feelings successfully or with much satisfaction, I refused to put aside or negate my experience. I felt that if I had the opportunity to relate in a creative expressive manner, I could convey my experience: my feelings, thoughts, and my new understanding of life. But, since I did not have the verbal ability or creative opportunities to express my intimate, in-depth thoughts, I just smiled and repeated "Life is beautiful."

During recuperation, following my stay in the hospital, my poor ability to verbally communicate feelings and thoughts prevented me from reality-testing my ideas concerning myself and others. Seven months after my accident I began traveling around the country alone to discover who I was and where I wanted to go in my life: personally, professionally, and spiritually.

My deeply illuminating experience of life subsequent to the coma state remained with me for over six months. It was a physiological and psychological way of knowing myself as well as a new sense of the world. I felt a purpose in my life, an understanding of why I was living, which I was able to sense but could not verbalize. This sense had no similarity to an emotional feeling or mental cognition, but was a total mind-body-spirit intuitive awareness.

A year after my accident, seeking a means to acknowledge and communicate my awareness and feelings, I channeled my personal expression through the creative arts. Daily, I would write, draw, or paint my feelings and thoughts. Through reflecting on my creative process I felt an increased awareness and understanding of my life. It was this personal encounter that led me in new directions of learning and experience, and inspired me to develop a creative process in working with dying patients.

PART THREE: CREATIVE ARTS THERAPY
FOR THE DYING PATIENT
AND CONCERNED INDIVIDUALS

Creative arts therapy with dying patients and their families or other concerned individuals is a very important therapeutic process. This process fosters communication, especially in sensitive areas, by methods that are less threatening than direct verbal confrontation. It also alleviates some of the initial fear and embarrassment individuals may have in expressing themselves verbally in a dialogue. The creative arts therapy techniques discussed within this chapter focus on using art media and various themes to help a person verbally and nonverbally relate feelings and thoughts in a non-threatening, self-expressive manner.

Creative arts therapy facilitates spontaneous and personal expression that comes from within the conscious and unconscious, allowing for a flow of feelings and thoughts. This approach promotes the expression of feelings that are otherwise difficult to acknowledge verbally. Through drawing, sculpting, and painting, individuals can relate ideas and thoughts to themselves and others. Often, in art therapy sessions, many personal feelings about dying are uncovered and discussed openly. This process also facilitates a sharing of those feelings and thoughts between the patient and family members (or other involved individuals) which are difficult to discuss because of traditional labels and stigmas. Using different themes in which to focus creative expression and verbal exchange, the patient and family members share thoughts, feelings, and personal experiences in their lives.

Creative arts therapy sessions can be used to encourage communication, obtain insight, and nurture actualization of self-identity during the patient's final days. From my experience, as an expressive therapist working with elderly and dying patients, I have formulated several concepts and techniques. These creative arts therapy techniques are still evolving as I continue my work.

The art therapy process can first begin between the patient and therapist, helping the patient share feelings and thoughts verbally and nonverbally about his life and parting from life and loved ones. Secondly, therapeutic intervention with the family, apart from the patient, is recommended. This intervention is designed to assist the family to express feelings about the dying patient, feelings of loss and/or denial, and personal feelings of the dying process. Thirdly, it is important that art therapy sessions be set up with the patient and family and/or concerned individuals.

In this third aspect of therapy, the patient and family can communicate in verbal and creative-expressive (nonverbal) ways concerning:

A. The impending separation of the patient and family.
B. The patient's contribution to the family.
C. The family's relationship with the patient.
D. Thoughts and feelings concerning the family's past, present, and future.

This is a time of clearing up feelings and imparting personal gifts as the patient and family share words of wisdom or special feelings and thoughts.

The therapist should first discuss the expressive therapy process with participants to allay their fears and apprehensions, and set the conditions for honest and open communication. The potential benefits of expressive therapy at this critical time should be explained to family members and/or close relations intimately involved with the patient.

An important factor the therapist must note is the presence of physical handicaps which could hamper the patient from expressing himself in certain media. The therapist should also be aware that the patient may have a pending emotional need to express certain feelings. Thus the creative-expressive theme should evolve around the patient's current needs.

The creative theme is a point from which the patient and therapist may continue their verbal and nonverbal explorations. It is the author's opinion that therapists should not always confine themselves to the initial theme but rather develop the therapeutic theme to reflect the patient's deep feelings and needs. The theme should be open to change, to allow for a discussion of feelings and thoughts concerning the needs of the immediate situation.

When I begin working with a person, I first choose themes that facilitate awareness and insight into the patient's basic issues and conflicts. In subsequent sessions, themes stem from related material which is pertinent to the life of the patient and his family.

During several individual sessions I would ask the patient to develop a picture of:

1. yourself
2. your past life
3. your family and what you would like to give them
4. what you would like to give the world
5. what you did give your family and/or the world
6. "who you are" beneath the physical structure of yourself (spirit, soul, or psychological makeup).

Out of these six themes, the therapist and/or patient should decide which are the most critical and appropriate to use. The themes may be explored through whatever expressive medium the patient can relate to and work with. Allowances for new directions to be explored by the patient should also be made.

Working separately with the patient's family, the art therapy sessions can be structured around themes which may develop in the following order:

1. What does (or did) the patient mean to you? What part did he play in your life?
2. Can you relate verbally or express nonverbally in writing or drawing your feeling of loss?
3. What is or was the specific role of the patient in relation to your needs?
4. How will you satisfy and meet your needs which were previ-

ously met by the patient, without him in the new family structure?

Through the use of these themes, the art therapist strives to help the family confront and deal with issues of anger, dependence, and loss (just a few of the many possible issues) in a conscious, valuable, and personally satisfying way.

One of the goals of art therapy sessions with the patient and family (or involved individuals) together is to gain an acceptance and personal acknowledgment of the situation and to discuss the realities of the future for the family. Basic themes related to this goal are:

1. What type of relationship exists or existed between the patient and family?
2. What did you learn from this relationship?
3. What would you like to give each other to take on your personal journeys?

These themes allow for an emotional impetus toward a closer connection between the participant's feelings and sense of relationship to the people and issues at hand. The art therapy process can help bring a family and patient together in compassion and strength. Through this therapeutic process the fears of dying can be dispelled by an acceptance of the stages of life.

The therapeutic, expressive therapy process aids the patient and family as they deal with issues and feelings of dying, coping, and grieving, and brings to light basic and intricate thoughts and feelings. The art therapy processes I have described are not directed toward a goal of emotional catharsis nor do they make a personal judgment on a person's life. Instead, these processes uncover a sense of relationship to life and help the patient embrace the moments of dying with a clear mind, a full heart, and a deep sense of self.

BIBLIOGRAPHY

Dass, Ram and Levine, Stephan, <i>Grist for the Mill.</i> California: Unity Press, 1976.
Keleman, Stanley, <i>Living Your Death.</i> New York: Random House, 1974.
Kubler-Ross, Elizabeth, <i>Death, The Final Stage of Growth.</i> New York: Prentice Hall, 1975.
Kubler-Ross, Elizabeth, <i>On Death and Dying.</i> New York: First McMillan Paperback, 1969.
Moody, Raymond A., <i>Reflections On Life After Life.</i> New York: Bantam Books, 1977.
Moody, Raymond A., <i>Life After Death.</i> New York: Bantam Books, 1975.

IN MEMORIAM

Mr. O was a patient in a long-term care setting. For over a year he participated weekly in an art therapy group, until he was moved to another ward. He was transferred due to an administrative decision to bring a new patient onto his former ward. Three days after his move, Mr. O died. The explanation the doctors and nurses gave me—"He died of old age"—just seemed to be a pretense. This was a familiar excuse. But what I observed in Mr. O's case was that just the experience of moving from one ward to another ward could create enough confusion, despair, and upset for Mr. O to give up living.

This change in his living quarters from one ward to another represented not only an environmental change, but also a social and psychological change. The move meant a change in the staff Mr. O depended on and a change in the acquaintances and friends he relied on for socialization. Mr. O's death poses an important question. How many changes and losses can a man or woman stand before he or she gives up living? We do not just "die of old age." At times we may give up living.

I knew of another similar case where an elderly woman gave up her life. Julia, a participant in an adult day care program where I worked, was sent to the hospital for routine tests. She had begun to eat less and less and her family doctor recommended that she go to the hospital for evaluation. When she entered the hospital, the staff took away her dentures and placed them out of her reach, took her eyeglasses and put them where she couldn't find them, and took her clothes away, leaving her with only a white gown to wear. When I came to visit she was lying in bed wearing a skimpy, wrinkled, white gown, looking totally withdrawn and embarrassed about her condition. She stared at me but did not say anything.

In the adult day care program I would sing the Beatles' song "Julia" to her, but in the hospital, when I began to sing to her, she waved her hands in front of her face and said, "No, no." She then pointed upward and said, "I am going there." As I was leaving the hospital, I asked the nurse how Julia was doing. She said that so far all of her test results were negative, she showed no signs of illness, and would be probably going home in a couple of days. But I sensed something wrong with Julia. The next day she died. I felt that the shock of being in the hospital, stripped of her identity and self-esteem, was devastating to her. I could see the emptiness in her eyes and open mouth as she lay in her bed, waiting, just waiting.

Julia's daughter told me that her father had passed away in a hospital years before, and Julia might have felt that this was her time to die since she, too, was in the hospital. But the daughter commented sadly that she really did not know why Julia died.

Sometimes death touches us when it chooses and sometimes when we choose. Julia and Mr. O made their choices. But, did we really offer them an opportunity to continue to live a fulfilling life, or did they make their decision out of anguish and despair?

Section II:
The Experiential
Process

Chapter 7

Expressive Therapy:
A Pictorial Essay*

*If I would only always remember,
there is so much life to tap,
I'd never stop helping people to create.*

In 1972 I had a serious car accident which placed me in a coma
for fourteen days. Following weeks of therapy and care from my
family, I slowly recovered my physical and mental abilities. Subsequent to the accident I experienced a perfection in life which I could
not explain. I would express this by saying, "Life is beautiful" in a
slow, repetitive, contemplative fashion.

Seven months after the accident, I regained my normal patterns of
life. I then began to travel around the country, searching for my
identity, my path. I now see this quest as similar to the experiences
of elders and the disabled who have been shaken by the trauma of an
accident, emotional crisis, or illness, and are searching for meaning
and identity in their lives.

My work as an expressive therapist with elders and the disabled
reaffirms the enlightening experience I had after I awoke from my
coma. Life then was suddenly beautiful and perfect. For me, relating to elders and the disabled in their difficult times creates a feeling
of compassion and unity with all people who strive to touch, love,
appreciate, and be appreciated in their own way. In this pictorial
essay, as in my work, I reaffirm that we are not searching to realize
our potential but are in fact realizing ourselves, and developing ac-
cordingly. We can feel accepted, loved, and cherished for who we
already are.

I see life as a journey starting from where we are to who we truly
are.

---

*This chapter was previously published by the author under the title *Creative Arts
Therapy with Elders: A Pictorial Essay,* © 1978.

111

Photo by Nancy Rodgers

The experiences of a man, reflected through his hands.

A tale in quiet movement that roars from the fingers of elders.

His pen moves slowly across the paper. His eyes follow close behind. He finishes, settling back into his seat to stare at the picture as if it might move or give birth to something new. His facial expression remains the same while his eyes reveal changes in his inner experience. He reaches for a different color of pen and draws another picture. His mind dances with images. Words seem not to be needed. Memories, thoughts, feelings of his life come alive on his paper. He is a member of the expressive therapy group involved in self-discovery, expression, and exploration.

* * *

The expressive therapy process demonstrated in this essay involves the use of spontaneous drawing and painting. The participants are elders and the disabled who live in a long-term care facility. Their ages range from thirty to ninety-three. They suffer from physical and emotional handicaps due to strokes, cancer, alcoholism, depression, and other debilitating illnesses.

The weekly expressive therapy sessions were open to everyone in the hospital. The emphasis was on personal expression and exploration; participants interacted in a fervor of drawing, painting, talking, and singing. From five to thirty men and women attended each session. The majority of participants were mildly to severely confused, regressed, or withdrawn; some were aphasic and others blind. Within the group each individual was accepted and given support by other members. No one seemed different. No one was an outcast. Everyone related in his or her own way, at his or her own pace. Still, the elder and disabled participants seemed isolated, without a familiar home, with only memories and a daily hospital routine to console them. They are as strangers in a strange land, looking for love, compassion, and a sense of themselves.

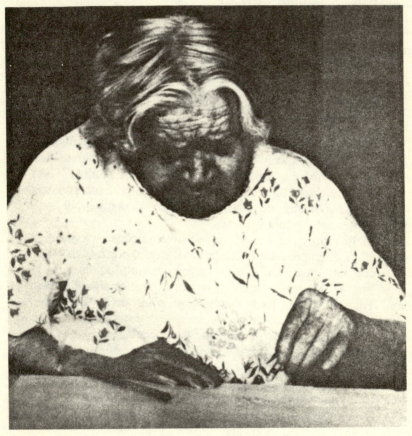

Photo by Nancy Simone

As the expressive therapist, I supplied art materials, music, a caring relationship, and rapport. I was the facilitator, a conductor of the group process, aiding each person in self-expression, communication, and sharing. In the group we talked, drew, painted, sang, touched, held each other, laughed, and cried while portraying our feelings. With a mere glance and an expressive drawing, years of love, sorrow, and hope were conveyed.

Elders who I thought were stiff,
Move gracefully at the touch of a pen.
Elders who never spoke,
Repeat the words they write.
Elders who seemed comatose,
Open their eyes at the sight of colors.
Isolated elders,
Suddenly touch each other.
A wealth of life slowly spun
From the elders' arms and hands,
As they move their brushes against the paper.
This isn't just art therapy
It's a gift of God.

The following pictorial essay of elders and the disabled involved in their creative process is sequenced to convey the participants' feelings, group processes, and creative experiences. Within these experiences are the dynamics of self-encounter—awareness, reflection, reorientation, and assertion. Through this process each individual also enhanced his sense of pride and self-esteem. The hidden reservoir of meaning and experience in each person's life was reflected in his activities. The participants expressed little in words, but their graphic expression and nonverbal communication conveyed a whole world.

The following essay is notated with my commentary: observations, feelings, and events. I find the words are truly not mine, but are acknowledged, accepted, and expressed by the participants themselves. I take the credit for observing elders and the disabled creating their own beautiful life-transforming experience.

To the jewels of still time—
   the lonely hearts in grey shadows,
   the hungry people of the city.
To the quiet hours in the country,
   where your footsteps are your only conversation.
To the men of time who are too weak to cry.
To those who weep for love and loss,
   old photos instead of friends.
To the stars that do not glow.
To the heart that is covered with dust.
To those confused, in despair,
   no place to turn, no one to care.

To the death-still hours
   I still find crowds.

Photo by Nancy Simone

Often elders and the disabled feel their lives as impoverished. While trying to cope with their changing life circumstances, they inadvertently neglect and lose meaning of their inner feelings. In expressive therapy, one emphasis is on the inner life.

Photo by Nancy Simone

I paint my experience

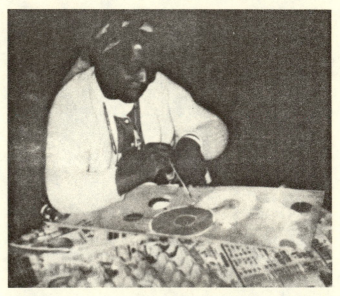

the universe,

my world among worlds,
my life among others.

A participant of ''Pleasure
Endeavors'' art therapy group.

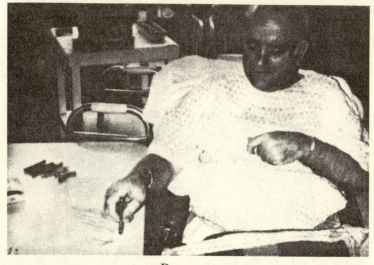

By crayon

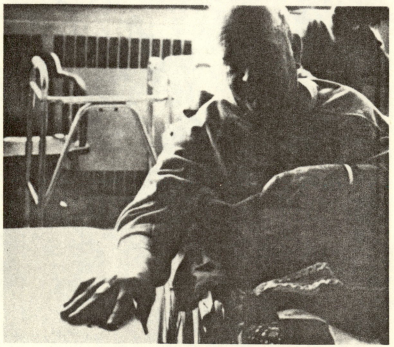

or by finger
it's the same heart speaking.

Photo by Nancy Rodgers

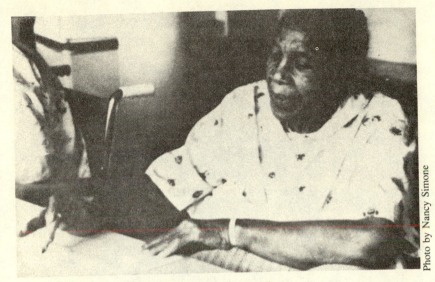

Photo by Nancy Simone

Gracefully like a dove

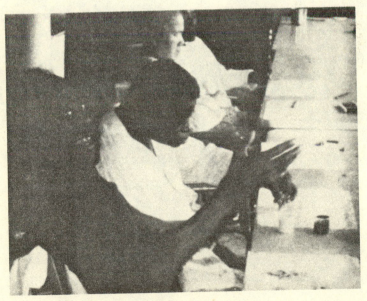

and light as a joke,
do I sometimes tell my story.

I write words,
the constitution of my soul.

Photo by Nancy Simone

I draw a castle,
that shines in the sun,
A castle with knights,
white towers and colored images.
A castle with one Queen.

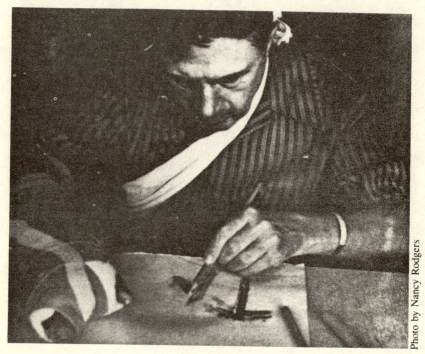

Photo by Nancy Rodgers

The study.

How deeply feelings move me
when I touch the paper.

Photo by Nancy Rodgers

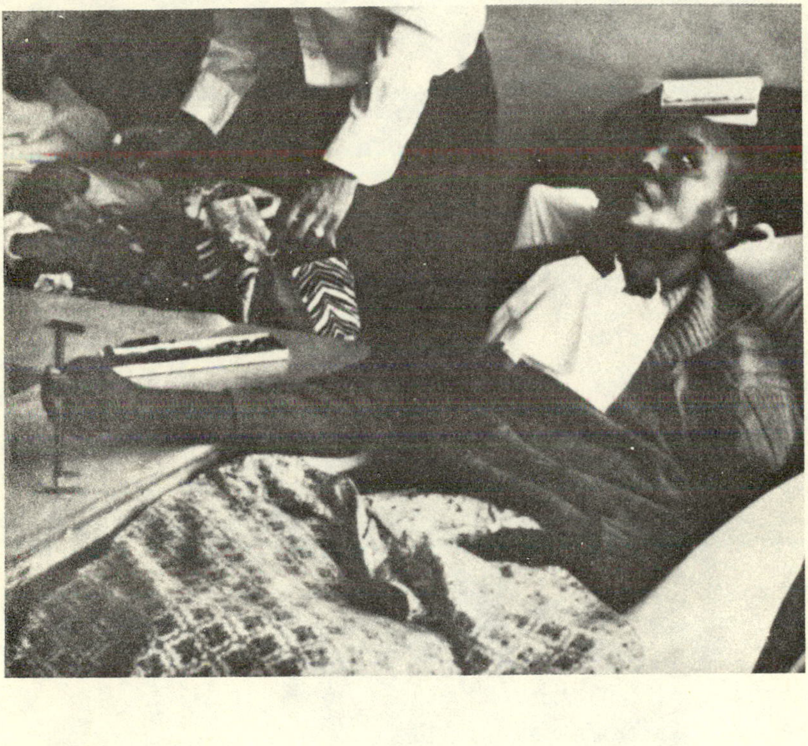

Photo by Nancy Rodgers

To contemplate,

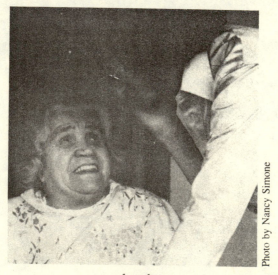

Photo by Nancy Simone

laugh,

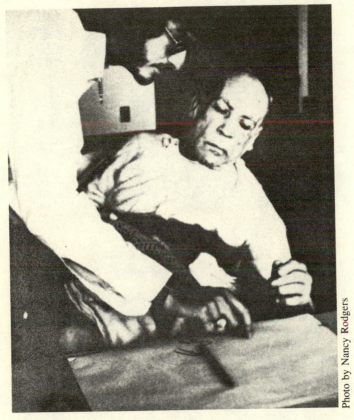

and share.

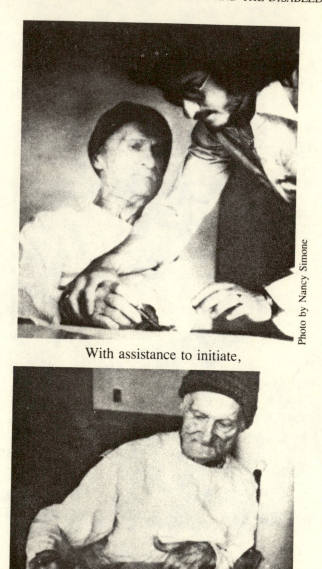

Photo by Nancy Simone

With assistance to initiate,

a whirlwind of motion and emotion

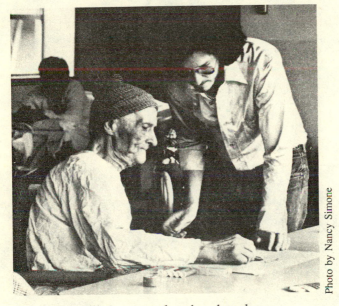

Photo by Nancy Simone

till the sea calmed and spoke.

Photo by Nancy Simone

Watching is creating:
thoughts, feelings.

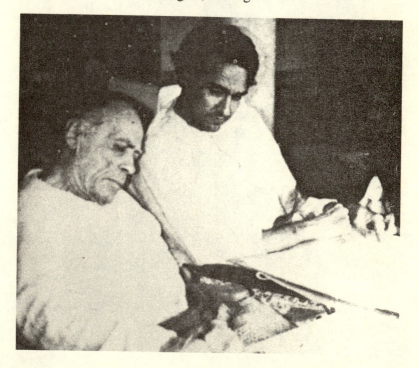

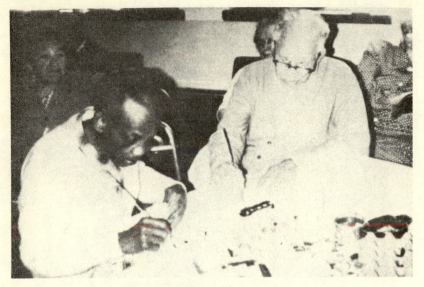

Thoughtfully, with care,
we speak silently, and reflect.

We share the pictures, images
of what we feel and think.

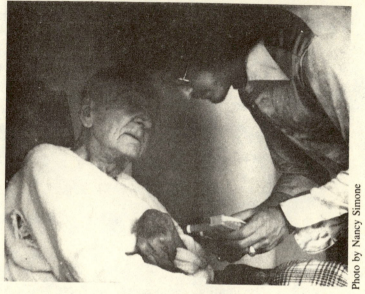

Photo by Nancy Simone

A lone rider
on a stormy night.

Photo by Nancy Simone

I explore

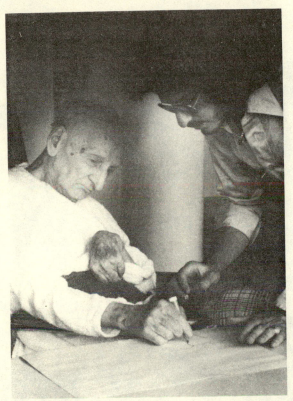

Photo by Nancy Simone

The trees are strong,
and the air warm.
I write words expressing
a journey that is beyond my thoughts.
A journey in the night,
crossing the desert.
A journey in mountains and valleys.
A journey of sorrow and laughter.
A journey of life.

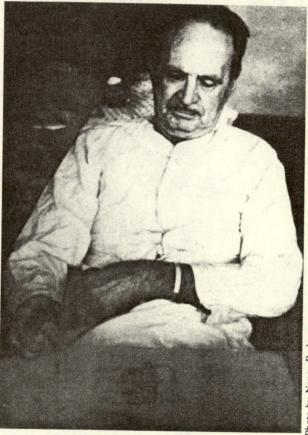

Photo by Nancy Rodgers

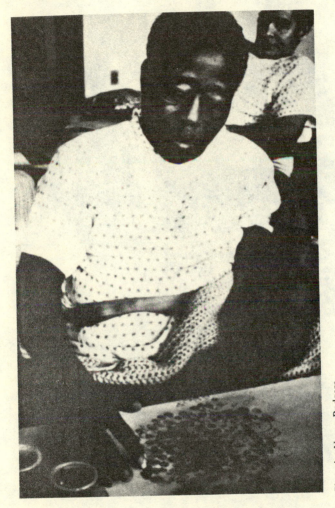

Photo by Nancy Rodgers

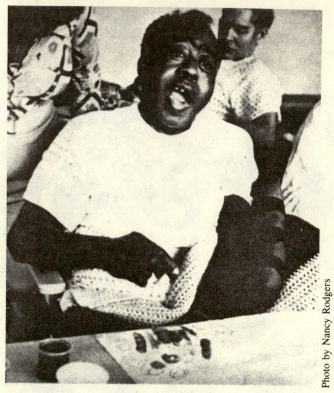

Photo by Nancy Rodgers

To you I sing,

Together we draw,

With you
we share.

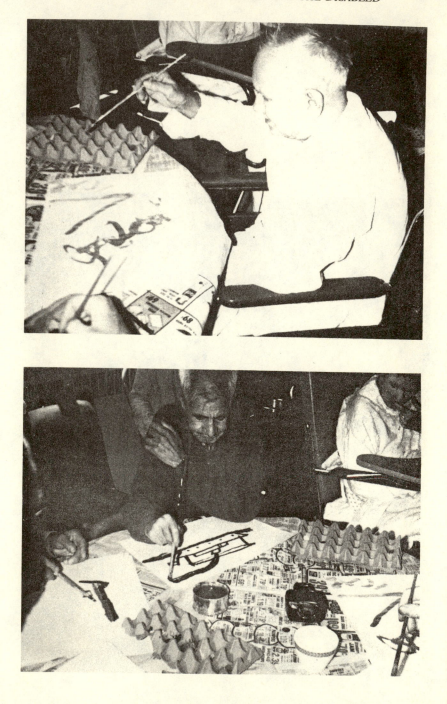

We join in a quiet repose,
creating a picture.
Telling of our day,
laying out the cards of our life
with each stroke of the brush.

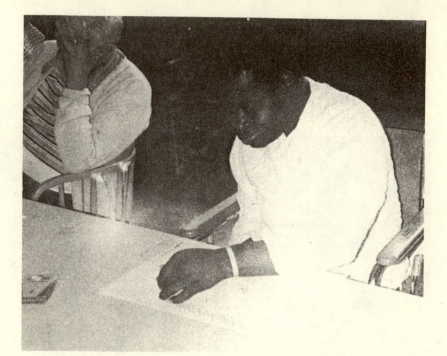

By myself, to myself,

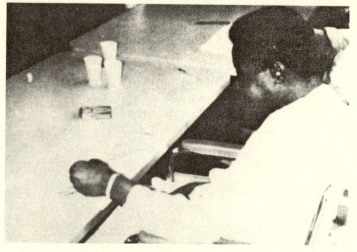

with myself

and you.

A joy beyond all thought,
all understanding,
A glow of warmth radiates
like the colors of the rainbow,
shading the days of my life,
reflecting in all my ways.

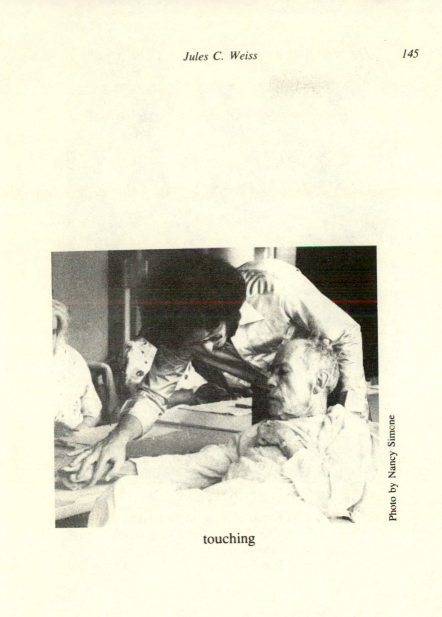

touching

Photo by Nancy Simone

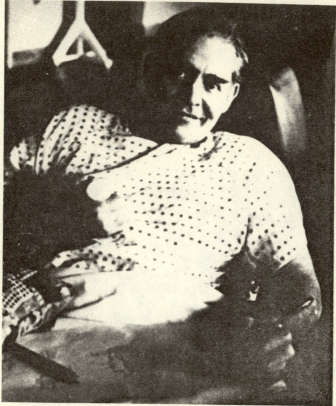

Photo by Nancy Rodgers

People think and hope about the future.
They live their lives wondering about tomorrow,
often missing today in the dizziness of a wishful hope.
An elder's tomorrow is today.
An elder's dream is the present.
An elder's hope is living.
An elder's wish is now.
An elder has nowhere else, but to be here, now.
Who will be with him?
Who will stop busying themselves with tomorrow,
to share with an elder's today?
Who will see in the face of an elder
a reflection of himself, in future days.
Who has forgotten this life is but a process?
Not the elder!
Who will remember and still smile at you.

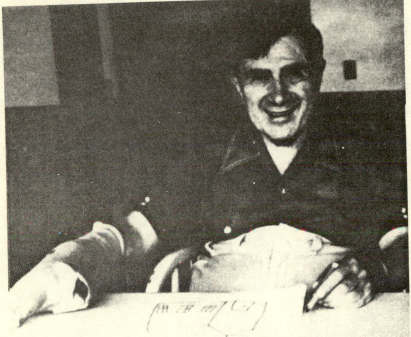

Photo by Nancy Simone

A man who loves and brings a gift to give
is totally different.
The physical part looks the same.
The gift may not be of any value;
it may be just a flower plucked by the side of the road—
an ordinary flower—
but he comes and presents it . . .
When he gives, he gives with totality.
And he is happy that his gift has been accepted.
He feels grateful that his gift has not been rejected.
He thanks the receiver.
He had been dreaming, fantasizing
about the moment when he would give it.

Bhagwan Shree Rajneesh
*The True Sage**

Chapter 8

The Creative Product:
An Expression of Feelings, of Thoughts,
and of One's Soul

The creative product reflects the feelings, thoughts, and ambiance of the creator. Often elders and the disabled will participate in Creative Arts Therapy to express, explore, and reflect upon their lives. They ponder about their pasts, wondering what would have happened if they had done something differently. They question who they are now and how they got to the present day. They imagine what will happen to them or consider how they can make their future better. The creative process can assist elders and the disabled in gaining new perspectives through sharing their feelings, thoughts, and memories. It enables them to create from their sense of being.

The following pages of photographs of paintings and drawings done by elders and the disabled are the reflections of the thoughts and feelings of men and women. People similar to those you may know, who have smiled and laughed with you, share their inner feelings through their paintings, drawings, and writings. Aspects of the individual which previously may have been hidden from the eye are felt, revealed, and reflected within the creative product. Similar to seeing a person's physical reflection in a pond, a drawing, painting, writing, or collage is a reflection of the inner soul. A drawing or painting not only exemplifies the individual perspective or attitude of a given moment, but also shares and uncovers the feelings and thoughts of a whole person, of a life. As it is said, the Almighty created us in His image and so do we create in the image of our feelings and thoughts.

The pictures within this chapter are not just photos of mere drawings, writings, and paintings, but are glimpses of roads walked by souls who have lived, loved, experienced, and shared in life. All drawings, paintings, and writings, were done by elderly and disabled people who live in a long-term care/rehabilitation hospital. The art work and writings were created in art therapy groups which I facilitated. The commentary on these pictures, written by the author, is in recognition of the participants' psycho-social experiences and expressions. It is a road we all may walk someday.

I came to the
hospital. . .

"ABCDEFGHIJKLMNOPQRSTUVWXYZ
I came to the hospital by train. I travelled so fast
I passed a lot of scenery, then fell
asleep so that's all I remember.''

My room feels strange,
I feel strange.

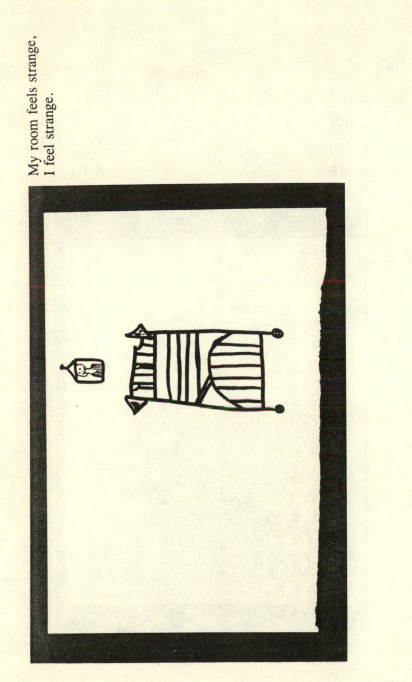

I meet another person,
but our arms can't
reach to touch.

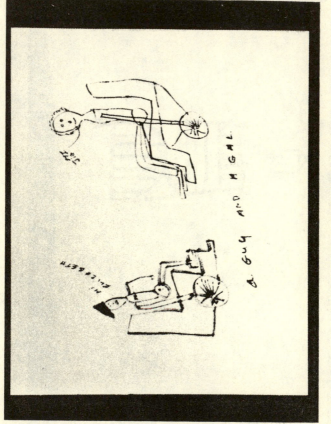

"Hi Elizabeth" "Hi Jim"
"a guy and a gal"

I feel lonely,
like the first
man on earth.

"Adam the first man on earth
that is why he looks lonely and
looking for someone to make him happy."

I have my struggles.

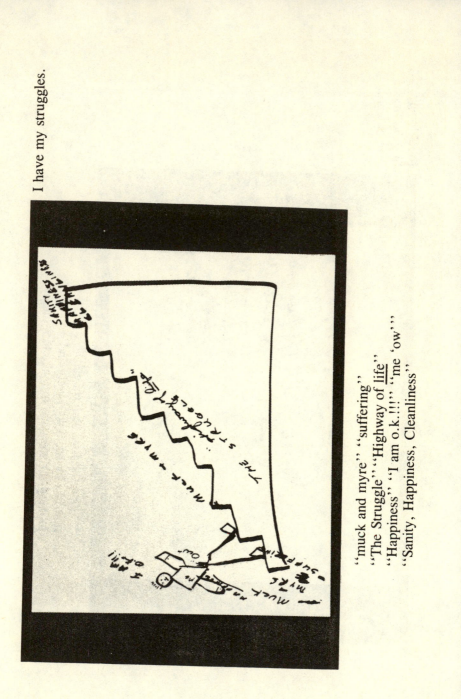

"muck and myre" "suffering"
"The Struggle" "Highway of <u>life</u>"
"Happiness" "I am o.k.!!!" "me 'ow'"
"Sanity, Happiness, Cleanliness"

I realize my pain.

Today I Feel Fair

I Don't Feel good, A BETTER Situation

BETTER.

I Loved my Wife in Better Times

She is Dead

"Today I feel fair
I don't feel good, a Better situation
Better.
I loved my wife in Better times
She is Dead."

I feel my inner beast.

"Beast"

I feel my different faces,
my different feelings.

I question myself,
but feel no time to
find out.

"How i see it now
is a phony,
you name it
Jap-Hawain
Cleopatra?
No Time To Find Out."

I have fears of the world.

The Rainbow, the sun
and the moon. Coming together,
on a Dar Knight
the world be
coming to an end.

"The rainbow, the sun, and the moon,
coming together on a dark night
the world be coming to an end."

I am troubled inside.

I have my needs. . .
It is like a jail here
in the hospital.

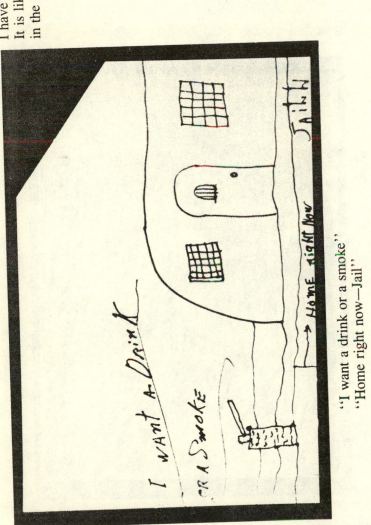

"I want a drink or a smoke"
"Home right now—Jail"

I think of my past.

"China"

I think of the beauty
I have seen
and I feel calm.

I fantasize about a home
I call "relief."

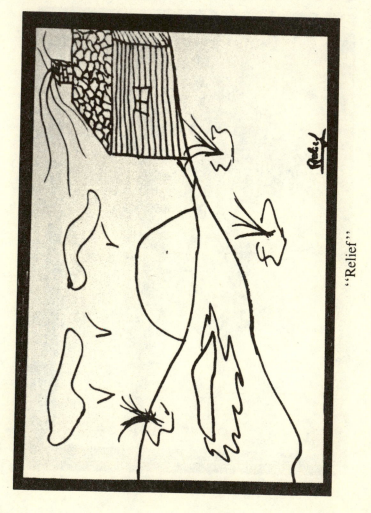

"Relief"

I think of my home.

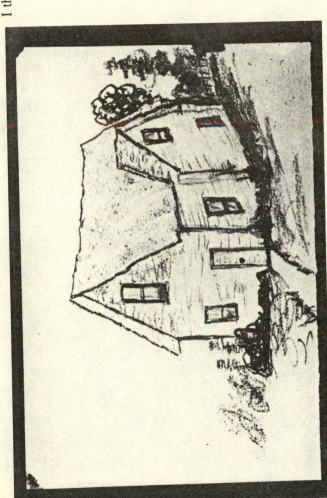

Time seems disturbed
in a hospital
and at my age.

I think of my final peace.

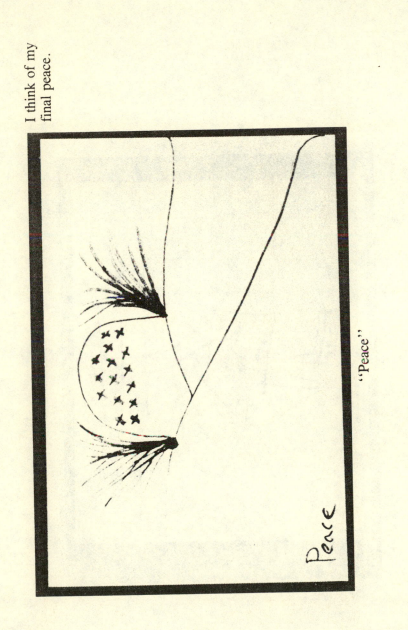

"Peace"

My goal is good

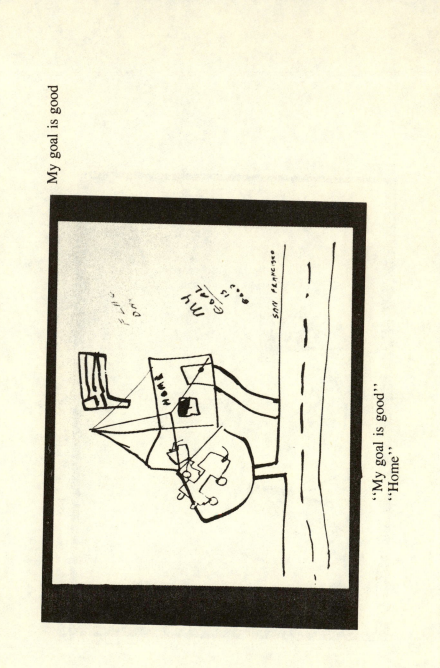

"My goal is good"
"Home"

I have feelings.
I have thoughts.
I am full.
I am whole.
I am who I am.
I feel good about myself.

Section III:
The Conceptual
Framework

Chapter 9

Touching the Heart of Therapy

People who work in the helping profession often develop a particular perspective based upon their training and personal experience. During my work as an art and activity therapist in a long-term care facility, I searched for the meaning of peoples' lives as I interacted with, listened to, and observed their daily struggles. Through this endeavor, I discovered that life does support and love us, just as we are. Even if we are disabled and/or growing old, our lives still have deep meaning and we can retain our connection to a healthy life.

From the insight and understanding gained during my years of professional work, I developed nine principles which I feel lie at the heart of the therapeutic process. These principles are grouped into three categories: General Context; Communication and Sharing; Insight and Perception. Within this chapter, I will describe the nine principles and their application to the therapeutic process.

These insights do not originate from scholastic study or experimentation with various styles and techniques of therapy, but rather come from giving, sharing, understanding, and being with people in acceptance and love. Although this context may have some similarities to other therapies, it is not drawn from any specific resource other than the understanding I found through my work.

The following principles are based on an understanding which we each can find and develop in our work with people. These insights can enable us to refine and clarify our communication, awareness, relationship to others, and enhance the quality of life we share and live.

A. General Context

1. Experience each person from the context of his life with acceptance and love.
2. Experience each person as perfect in his own way, just as he is.

3. Use your mind and work from your heart.

B. Communication and Sharing

4. Communicate with your heart and see each person from his heart.
5. Acknowledge that every person has the opportunity for vast potential in his life; share the feeling that each person's potential is found in the present moment.

C. Insight and Perception

6. Acknowledge that every person has the ability to experience, understand, and develop within the context of his life.
7. Acknowledge that every person is in control of his life to the extent that he is willing to be aware of and take responsibility for his life.
8. Recognize that every person is composed of the child, the adolescent, and the young, middle-aged, and older adult.
9. Perceive all experiences as opportunities for growth.

In the development of these principles, I discovered that when I did not only focus on the patients' illnesses and limitations, but looked at their "hearts," their lives, who they were, I realized a new depth in my understanding and experience of people. I found that when I communicated heart to heart, others experienced me as I experienced them, with a greater acceptance and love. From this experience, I saw that people who were classified as blind could see, those who were aphasic could speak eloquently in their own manner, and regressed individuals could use verbal and nonverbal means to relate their feelings and thoughts.

Principle 1. Experience each person from the context of his life with acceptance and love.

Often people relate to situations and others with a preconceived set of concepts and expectations. In working with people I came to understand that the categories, labels, and judgments I placed on an individual often got in the way of my experience, understanding, and communication. When I allowed myself to forego these preconceptions and labels,* and greeted the person with acceptance and love, I found a new intensity of feeling and awareness being created between us and within the individual. By relating in a personal, unassuming, intimate manner, with acceptance and love, new horizons were opened within the relationship.

CASE STUDY

This principle was a major aiding factor in a case I consulted on while working in a psychiatric/rehabilitation hospital. A fellow staff member who was an occupational therapist came to me concerning a problem she had with one of her patients. She explained to me that she was working with a seventy-five year old man who was recovering from a spinal operation which left him with a general (upper and lower) paresis. He would not cooperate in occupational therapy and fought her on every suggestion she made, resisting both verbally and physically. She said that all he would talk about was how bad the world was and how he couldn't do anything anymore. In an angry tone of voice, he told her that he had been a very active man all of his life, until his operation. Now, since the operation, he was confined to a wheelchair with much loss of mobility and body functioning. He felt helpless, hopeless, and angry. To him the world was no good, he was no good, and he thought and felt that no one and nothing could help him.

The longer the patient resisted treatment, the more angry and frustrated the occupational therapist became. She tried to think of many different tasks for him to do, but he would always sabotage her efforts with negativity and anger. The occupational therapist felt she was failing him. She was also angry with him because he would not cooperate in treatment. When she came to me she said that she felt like giving up because there didn't seem to be anything she could do for him.

After I heard the story of the case I realized that the patient thought that others were not hearing his anger and feeling his frustration. The more he expressed his feelings and anger to the occupational therapist, the more she withdrew. This left him feeling more

---

*The author feels that medical and psychological background information concerning patients is a very important tool in therapy and is not to be neglected but rather used appropriately.

frustrated, angry, and isolated. He was angry about the injustice and unfairness of his situation, and felt frustrated and hurt because he thought he would be unable to live the life he had known prior to his operation. I felt that the patient first needed to express his feelings and acknowledge his situation. Then, he could clearly choose if he wanted to be helped.

I advised the occupational therapist to stop giving the patient tasks to do because the tasks were probably threatening to him. Due to his condition, he was unsure of his present worth and abilities and had many negative feelings about being disabled. He would likely interpret a failure in a task as a personal failure and as an example of how bad things were in his life. I saw that through his anger and frustration, he was verbally and nonverbally stating that he could not accept his disability.

I also advised her that, for a while, she should just let the patient talk about his life and his feelings concerning being disabled. I felt that the patient had a great need to express his anger and frustration to someone who would listen to him and accept him for how he felt, because he could not accept himself in his present condition.

The occupational therapist agreed with my evaluation and said that she would try the course of action I recommended. A few days later, she reported to me that in the next three sessions she only listened as he talked about his life. She did not initiate any other intervention. They began to form some trust and a feeling of closeness between them. In his fourth session she asked him, like a friend and as his therapist, ''What do you want to do next, begin in rehabilitation or stay the same?'' He answered the question in a positive frame of mind and decided to begin a program of active rehabilitation.

In this case, counseling was needed to assist the patient through his depression. Issues such as feelings of self-worth, importance and value to his family, friends, and society were some of the crucial factors that needed to be discussed and dealt with. In addition to her primary role as the occupational therapist, she acted as the patient's counselor. She helped him to begin to face and deal with his negative self-image and other barriers to his rehabilitation, while pacing the occupational therapy treatment program so he could experience some success in treatment to give him further hope in rehabilitation.

In my review of this case, I noted that at first the patient did not want help or assistance for his disability but, instead, wanted to be able to express his anger, feelings of injustice, and confusion and unsureness about his future. He wanted to be accepted for who he was, to feel that he was still a man and had a meaningful life to live. The need for rehabilitation was not the major problem blocking the patient's growth, but rather his feelings and thoughts concerning whether he could live as a handicapped person, and still be loved, appreciated, and valued.

I was notified by the occupational therapist that after several weeks of treatment in occupational therapy the patient increased his shoulder and elbow strength and learned to walk again with the use of a walker. He was becoming more active in his home and in the community and was working toward a healthy and satisfying adjustment to his new life.

Principle 2. Experience each person as perfect in his own way, just as he is.

Each person spends his life working, studying, relating to the world to finally reach this moment: the present. The present is a moment of perfection reflecting the individual's life. What is perfect about the present? The present is the totality of a person's accumulated experiences, wisdom, and understanding of life.

When I experience a person as "perfect" just as he is, I am then experiencing and accepting the individual unconditionally, no matter what disability he may have. The client who experiences unconditional acceptance from the therapist may begin to have an added sense of appreciation and love for himself.* This acknowledgment helps the individual to become more in touch with the inner self and to further recognize his feelings and express himself in all relationships. When a person acknowledges his life and feels acceptance and regard for it, then growth may occur more easily (the river finds the sea).

For a therapist to acknowledge and experience each person as he is, the therapist needs to see the client with an empathetic acceptance and understanding. This acceptance includes recognizing the client's perceptions of himself and of the world. The client's perceptions may be based on or influenced by various factors: how the client

---

*The experience of unconditional love may bring up various feelings for the client. Feelings which surface may include a need for acceptance, past feelings of rejection, or the feeling that the person has received undeserved love. Whatever may arise in the client's consciousness concerning this experience may be very important material to be dealt with between the therapist and client.

feels he should act; whether the client is trying to get approval from someone in his life; who the client feels he is, internally and socially; and other variables affecting the client's perceptions and feelings. Intimacy in a relationship is sometimes developed through acceptance and appreciation of the different perspectives and concepts the client has of the self while still relating to the "heart" of the individual.

I became aware of this principle while working as an art and activity therapist in a long-term care facility. Many of the patients felt an unspoken duty to participate in art projects and activities. There were several reasons the patients felt this way: to gain a friend on the staff level, to fit into the milieu so they could hope to have other needs met, or a perception that they had to go along with the program schedule to avoid difficulties with staff and patients.

When I realized that many patients were operating out of these feelings, I explained to them that they did not have to participate in activities to please me but could do what pleased them within the activity: whether it was to sit and watch others participate, or to become more involved in the group process. I felt a patient's sense of self-integrity, choice, and freedom was more important than having a large number of people at my activity. By allowing patients to choose their level of participation, I was offering them the permission to be themselves, and the freedom to participate at their own level, pace, and time. This helped me to relax my expectations of what should occur within the group session and gave me more freedom to create the session in a spontaneous manner. Through this process, participants began to interact with me and others within the group in a more authentic, honest, and intimate manner.

Principle 3. Use your mind and work from your heart.

We are given a heart and mind at birth. The mind works like a computer; thinking, storing facts, deciphering and figuring out our problems. The heart represents the emotional and spiritual aspects of ourselves: our feelings, empathy, and compassion; our relatedness to others, our love.

At times people forget their feelings, their connection to others, and relate only from their mind (the computer). People may think they know and understand another person but neglect the individual's feelings, experiences, and perspective. An Indian proverb says, "Do not criticize another person until you walk a mile in his shoes.'' In this sense it is important to know a person through your heart and feelings, and use your mind as you would use a computer: tame it, program it, and use it within its limits. For example, we may have difficulty dealing with a patient who is behaving in a way we can neither understand nor relate to. If we act only from our mind, or from our preconceptions, we may be ineffective. We must also use our heart and empathy to fully understand, feel, relate to, and act within the situation.

We know the world through our feelings and senses; we remember, recognize, and conceptualize our experiences through our mind. A basic precept for a healthy life is to *use* our mind and *live* from our heart. It is an old proverb; heart and mind must be in accord, it is the harmony of heaven and earth.

Principle 4. Communicate with your heart and see each person from his heart.

In my work with elders and the disabled I found that when I did not just focus on the pain, discomfort, or misfortune of the individual, his disability would not be the major focus of our relationship and interaction. By viewing a person from his heart, feelings, and life, I related to the love and magnitude of the individual, not just the person's limitations. Without this negative focus, I found that people would relate with a greater sense of self and an increased awareness of their strengths and abilities.

To communicate with one's heart means to share with another person, in a positive manner, one's feelings and sense of empathy. To see each person from his heart means to relate to the center of the person; not just to the individual's symptoms or problems, but to the primary source of the individual, the heart, the whole life.

The "heart-felt" process of relating is not always a conscious or verbal process. It could be described as two people sharing a warmth and mutual understanding, both verbally and nonverbally. To communicate with one's heart and see each person from his heart is a bridge to a new beginning; a new context or reference with which to relate to or perceive each other.

When one communicates from the heart and with a sense of empathy, opportunities for growth and enjoyment are created for both the patient and oneself. Through communicating in this manner the health-care worker is often perceived by the patient to be understanding and to have compassion and sincerity.

Principle 5. Acknowledge that every person has the opportunity for vast potential in his life; share the feeling that each person's potential is found in the present moment.

Many people grow up in life learning of their limitations and dreaming of fulfilling their potential. Too often we focus on our losses, our mistakes, instead of exploring the unknown world of our potential. Fear of failure, fear of not being "normal," and just plain fear, often rule peoples' lives and block their opportunities to explore their potential and live a fuller life. To live and fulfill one's potential, a person often needs to have trust and faith in oneself. It is also helpful to feel trust from the people a person interacts with and to feel secure in the environment.

People often have a need to fulfill the expectations of others, which can be a positive or negating growth experience. A child wants to fulfill the parents' expectations, and wives and husbands often act to fulfill each other's expectations. Patients in hospitals also often want to fulfill the staff's expectations. I have found that many people need and look for the attention and acceptance of others, even if it means compromising themselves or staying ill. In my work in hospitals and institutions I saw people fulfilling the expectations of others by trying to conform to the category or diagnosis in which they were labeled. In order to seek extra attention, patients would focus on their disability, thus fulfilling their own negative expectations.

Our society has low expectations of elders and the disabled. This is reflected in the typical negative connotations which are placed on these individuals. How often do you hear someone talk about the potential of elders and the disabled?

Although a person may have some disability or handicap, each person also has a range of abilities. People can use their many abilities to compensate for their disability. Everyone is disabled is some way, but we also have many other abilities to compensate for our disabilities. Every person needs to look at his abilities to see how he can grow and overcome any disability he may have. (This is not to negate the areas of disability which can use improvement.) A person can work toward developing himself to such an extent that his strength will be greater than his disability, whether this disability is physical, emotional, or mental. Through becoming aware of our strengths and abilities, we can find new avenues to express, explore, and enjoy life. We need to remember that our potential is limitless;

both our potential and limitations are created by ourselves and our beliefs.

Principle 6. Acknowledge that every person has the ability to experience, understand, and develop within the context of his life.

We are a many-faceted jewel carved by our own hands. Our life is composed of many variables and choices such as our wishes, desires, patterns of interaction and communication, accomplishments, and difficulties. Too often we may blame our fate on others or on circumstances. Circumstances and experiences can influence and/or teach us, depending on how we incorporate and use them. We create our lives; our personality and being are our own reckoning. As therapists we can point our clients to the fact that they are the master craftsmen of their lives.

Each person has a variety of experiences in life. The process by which a person interprets and relates to his experiences determines the quality of his life. There are times a person's experiences may seem to dictate his feelings. However, in perspective, we can see that our experiences only trigger our feelings, not dictate them. We can either be in harmony with our emotional experiences or controlled by them. This is true for people of all intellectual capacities, for emotions are not dependent on one's intellect. In this regard, people may begin to realize the responsibility they have in respect to their feelings, attitudes, and actions.

Everyone has the ability to experience, understand, love, and develop according to their needs, abilities, and wants. Personal experiences and individual concepts about life, people, and one's self can be viewed either as limitations to or as examples of one's freedom. The values, ideals, and perspective a person chooses to live by influences the awareness and potential of his life. Some people do not consciously choose certain personal values and perspectives but live by the values and perspectives of others. For example, patients in hospitals may take on the perspective and values of their caretakers. Health-care workers become very influential just by the nature of their job and their close relationship with patients.

People are sensitive to love, touch, sound, taste, verbal and nonverbal communication. The intellect of elderly and disabled individuals may appear to lose its potential because of various cognitive and/or social-emotional handicaps. However, the feeling ability of the individual is usually strong unless undue deadening has occurred due to an unhealthy physical, emotional, or spiritual environment. We often imagine, in our negative conditioning, that a person has fewer abilities than he actually possesses. So often we look at what a person has lost instead of looking at what he has. Even regressed individuals may have a strong and active capacity for feeling, although their verbal communication of feelings may seem confused. This is why therapeutic modalities such as art, music, and movement therapy are so important in developing communication and self-expression with regressed and nonverbal individuals. We need to encourage each person, no matter how little or great his disability or difficulty, to experience life and develop within his life structure and concepts.

CASE STUDY

This concept was clearly illustrated to me by Gus, a patient who lived in a long-term care facility where I worked as an art and activity therapist. He was a fifty-year-old man who was paralyzed from the waist down. He had minimal coordination due to a degenerative nerve disease and was dying of a brain tumor. His hands and fingers shook and he had extreme difficulty in holding or using an object requiring dexterity such as a pen, a cup, or a fork. Although Gus could not walk, had difficulty in talking, stuttered nervously, and lacked the muscle coordination to do most tasks, his manner exemplified a sense of self-esteem and self-respect. Through discussing his feelings and thoughts with the staff and fellow patients, Gus gained a positive sense of himself and a realistic sense of his situation. His true enjoyment of life was found in expressing a great joy and compassion, and in taking the opportunity to examine and share the background of his life with others.

Gus' Participation in the Art Therapy Group

When the patients in the art therapy group first met they were rather quiet, seldom talking. However, after a few sessions they began to enjoy listening to music, singing, laughing, drawing, playing around, and being boisterous. It took a few weeks before the patients knew each other well enough to become personal and intimate, and to take the opportunity to do new things within the group setting. Although these patients lived in the same ward, some for over a year, intimacy had not previously developed between many of them.

Some of the participants were regressed, aphasic, blind, deaf, and physically handicapped individuals. These were people who were often silent and withdrawn, trying to forget they were in a hospital; people who believed their past would come back and they would again live in their own homes; people who, at times, would deny they knew the person in the bed next to them to avoid further recognition and identification with the reality of living in a hospital. These were people who felt violated by the intrusion of the hospital staff and other patients' guests. People who felt sexless, in white hospital gowns, waiting, waiting, just waiting. These patients were Gus' peers, the people who surrounded his daily life.

In the ward Gus' interaction with other patients was often only for a moment during commercials on the blaring television sets which were found at every bed. It was important for Gus' health to "connect" with a fellow human being, to relate to someone, to recognize his life and the life about him. When Gus and other patients participated in the art therapy group, they met each other on equal grounds, without the distraction of televisions playing and the boundaries of each person's bed. In the art therapy group, patients had a chance to socialize, to meet each other in an intimate way, and relate and discuss their lives.

Although it was very difficult for him to even draw a five-line stick figure, Gus came regularly to the weekly art therapy group. What Gus really enjoyed in the group was not drawing (which I felt he did only to please me) but rather his chance to interact with other patients and myself, sharing his feelings and thoughts.

As the group therapist, I would often ask Gus to introduce new members to the group, or begin a discussion, or talk about the art created by group members. Here Gus took a leading role, inspiring and encouraging others to draw, talk, and interact. Gus welcomed each member to the group and politely asked them how they were (even asking the patients who were deaf and/or aphasic). In a soft voice he described the group objective to new members and offered art materials for them to use. In this role Gus was not an ill patient but rather a host, a friend, a person interested in being a companion to others. Gus talked about his past with the group, describing his schools days, the girls he went out with, and his previous jobs. He shared the truth of his life with others within the group and they did the same.

In the art therapy group Gus was beginning to develop his relationship with staff and fellow patients, using the group as a focus for his social communication and interaction. Though Gus' peers usually acted withdrawn and quiet (feeling the stresses and problems of their past and present life) Gus reached out to them in a manner which showed he also knew when to respect a fellow patient's privacy. Gus' interest in relating to patients and staff created a sense of mutual strength, compassion, and acceptance.

Gus created a fulfilling life for himself through sharing his feelings and thoughts. Giving Gus some direction and encouragement seemed to be my role as the activity therapist. His potential manifested in his acceptance, enjoyment, and appreciation of life, while respecting and caring for each person with whom he interacted. He gave others a sense of being ''okay.'' This sense is very important, especially in a hospital where patients may never feel ''okay'' about themselves unless they are made aware of their worth. Gus was fulfilling his potential in the art therapy group by sharing who he was, listening to others, and creatively and enjoyably interacting with everyone.

Principle 7. Acknowledge that every person is in control of his life to the extent that he is willing to be aware of and take responsibility for his life.

We have choices at all moments—choices of how to act and react. At times we may feel we are reacting compulsively or instinctually. During other times, we acknowledge the choices we have and possibly the resistance, avoidance, and/or discomfort we have in consciously making these choices. A common ritual for excusing behavior is to explain, ''I was brought up that way'' or ''No one told me differently.'' These excuses do not refute our responsibility to ourselves or to others.

Patients may ask others to take responsibility for their actions, especially if they are unsure of themselves. However, each individual needs the opportunity to take responsibility for and act upon his own life. In some cases, unfortunately, the health-care worker can take the opportunity of free choice away from the patient by making choices and decisions for the individual. In this regard, there is a fine line between helping a person and making a person dependent on your help.

As we are aware of the choices and the controls we have in our life, we become aware of our personal power. This power gives us a sense of vitality and connection to this ever-changing life. Our power comes from our ability to respond at will to the situations in our life; to express our feelings and acknowledge our thoughts. Our personal power stems from having a positive sense of self. We are in control of our life to the extent that we are aware of our life and can respond authentically by our feelings, thoughts, and actions.

Principle 8. Recognize that every person is composed of the child, the adolescent, and the young, middle-aged, and older adult.

As we grow up we leave behind our toys, our adolescent crushes, our high school days, our youthful romances, our first job experiences, and so forth. However, we do not need to exclude those aspects of ourselves which are in our memories and in our hearts. By using the information and feeling level of every growth period we have gone through, we may enrich our life by incorporating the experiences of our past.

Too often people look away from the past because of painful memories, or due to the feeling that they are "supposed" to act grownup. To be in touch with one's life and joy, one needs to be in touch with one's pain. To be in touch with the adult self, one needs to be in touch with the child within. We do not leave behind our past like a forgotten parcel, but we incorporate our past into our present life, producing a healthy, whole person.

Often people become stuck in the "serious adult self" and have trouble laughing and playing because these actions may appear childish. Joy in those people's lives is often noticed by a slight smile. They do not laugh with their belly and shake their body in joy, but rather produce a controlled smile or chuckle, and possibly a twinkle in their eyes. I do not feel that there is any ultimate salvation in laughter or joy, but it is healthy, fun, and fulfilling to be in touch with one's good feelings, especially in a playful and joyful way. Besides, it feels good to laugh and have fun. Why do we take everything so seriously with a frown? Why not take it seriously with a smile and laugh, and uplift oneself without avoiding one's feelings?

Being in touch with the feeling of joy may remind people of their childhood: a childhood which they may be trying to avoid or grow out of. Often if we look at what a person is not feeling or expressing, we notice the areas in which he or she is blocked from joy and pain. We may find disembodied parts of the self longing for acceptance and feeling. If we look at the parts of the self which are in need, we are drawn to examine the different feelings of the individual's past and present which may be forgotten, neglected, or unresolved. These feelings may include "childish fears," "adolescent embarrassments," or other feelings which may recur in one's past and present life. By blocking out parts of the self, a person disregards and negates his primary experience, feelings, and concerns. To have a person reduce the self to the "serious adult," with no feelings for other aspects of the self, makes a person into an "adult machine." If we want to live fully we need to be fully in touch with the different aspects of the self: the child, the adolescent, and the young, middle-aged, and older adult.

We may act like adults at times and we may act like children at times. We can feel with sincerity and personal value the years of growth, pain, and joy in our life. We can cherish the memories and feelings of our past, and recreate them in the present to feel our joys, our needs, our love, and our connection to the life we have lived.

Principle 9. Perceive all experiences as opportunities for growth.

No matter where you are, who you are, and what you are going through, you can use the present moment as an opportunity for growth. Experiences can foster feelings, thoughts, insights, and relationships. The way a person abstracts or conceptualizes an experience, in either a positive or negative light, significantly changes the meaning, value, and feeling of the encounter. An experience gives information about a person or situation. The experience in itself is not a judgment but is rather a physical-emotional-cognitive relationship and situation. As a spiritual teacher once said,

> There is no dilemma in any experience
> there is only experience.
> Dilemma is the avoidance of experience.
> Dilemma questions, thinks, avoids the
> relationship of the experience.
> Experience and relationship must be total
> or else it is dilemma.
> The only fullness is in being.[1]

This and every other moment is your opportunity to feel, see, act,

---

[1]John, Da Free. *The Method of the Siddhas.* Middletown, California: The Dawn Horse Press, 1978.

and be who you are, where you are. The greatest value in your experience of life is in having the personal power to participate, create, and love in the present moment. Experiences are often a mirror of one's conscious and unconscious thoughts, feelings, and patterns of relationships. Reflecting upon your experiences can be a validation of what you gave, received, and learned.

*   *   *

A man in his fifties, who was a secretary at the long-term care facility where I held art therapy groups, came to me one day during a group session. He said that he was inspired by watching the elderly and disabled patients painting and creating art work and never realized that these people could create such beautiful pieces of art. He told me that he had stopped painting over thirteen years ago, but, seeing the elderly and disabled patients paint and create art work gave him the inspiration and fervor to start painting again. He said that he had bought new canvasses, paints, and brushes, and in two weeks had completed several paintings. He thought it had great therapeutic value for him, as he presumed it must have for the patients in the hospital. He exclaimed that he was very happy to once again be involved with an ongoing creative experience that gave further meaning, pleasure, and enjoyment to his life.

This situation exemplifies the idea that a stone thrown in a pond creates ripples that influence far and wide. As the patients expressed themselves through art, they created a sense of intimacy and community between themselves and with the staff. The staff had also changed in a positive manner as they participated in the patients' self-expressions, and development of community.

All experiences are opportunities for growth; even to watch others can bring us awareness of our life and the feelings and experiences we hold and create.

*   *   *

A troubled man once came to seek advice from a sage. The troubled man told the sage all of his problems and misfortunes and asked the sage to show him a pathway out of his misery. The sage was silent until the troubled man finished talking. He then said to the troubled man, "If the present moment is not perfect, then what is?

and if you do not learn from this experience then from what experience will you learn?'' The man then understood and walked away, feeling complete.

IN CONCLUSION

The nine principles previously mentioned are aids to an approach to therapy and relationships which is guided by one's heart, awareness, and sense of self. This approach was designed to aid health-care workers in the therapeutic processes they use with clients and to provide an enlightening context, or reference, to work by. Therapy is not something we do, but rather a process we participate in.

Awareness of Who We Are

The process of being.
We are here already.
There is no search,
There is only being.
Belonging to your path,
To your life.
The ultimate answer is you.
At your footstep.
We are here.
Look around.
Watch the trees.
Feel the air.
Refresh yourself.
You belong to life.
You are here.
You made it.
Be with yourself.
The search has only begun
And the answer is only felt
When you reach
The place
Just to be,
Yourself.
One with all
All with one.

BIBLIOGRAPHY

John, Da Free. *The Method of the Siddhas.* Middletown, California: The Dawn Horse Press, 1978.

Joy, W. Brugh. *Joy's Way—A Map for the Transformational Journey.* Los Angeles, California: J.P. Tarcher, Inc., 1979.

Moss, Richard. *The I That Is We.* Millbrae, California: Celestial Arts, 1981.

Chapter 10

Whole-Life Growth and Health Program for Residential Care, Long-Term Care, and Day Treatment

We are all chronic, steeped in our ways, wearing blinders. Who are we to classify another as limited? What do we truly know of our potential? Very little. But we know our limitations well.

Who are we to judge another person as being at their level of potential? In our humbleness we must agree, that we are the blind leading the blind in discovery of ourselves.

We can lead with utmost courage, enthusiasm, awe, and reverence for the potential each person has. There is so much for us to discover together; not just to know, but to be.

To treat a whole person we must address and relate to the full needs of the individual. Any given problem replicates itself throughout a person's life. If we cure the symptoms of a problem, there is a possibility that further symptoms may cease to manifest. However, patterns of dysfunctional, maladaptive, negative, and self-destructive behavior often reappear in many facets of a person's life and need to be treated through a wholistic reintegration of the self.

People who live in residential or long-term care facilities, or who participate in day treatment programs, often have a need for a variety of psycho-social activities, creative therapeutic interventions, and programs for learning ADL (activities of daily living). The Whole-Life Growth and Health Program focuses on meeting this wide spectrum of needs through a variety of activities, experiences, and therapeutic approaches and processes. A major goal of the program is to help participants discover and learn how to improve the quality of their lives.

The Whole-Life Growth and Health Program is designed as a wholistic program that includes the use of therapeutic modalities which engage and help to develop the many vital aspects of the "whole person" (such as the social, psychological, physical, and spiritual aspects). The therapeutic modalities are divided into six categories:

A. Expressive Therapy
B. Psycho-Social Activity Program
C. Verbal Therapy (Group and Individual)
D. Lifeskills Learning Program
E. Cultural and Social Program
F. Homecare Program

The first three categories (A, B, and C) are programs which both help the individual gain a greater sense of self and provide a range of ego-supportive experiences. Categories D, E, and F are psycho-social-physical "lifeskills" programs which provide for personal needs, self-care, and mental, physical, and social nourishment. These programs play a valuable and vital part in each person's rehabilitation, ongoing health, happiness, and personal development.

Category A, Expressive Therapy, involves Art, Movement, Music, Drama, Poetry, and Occupational Therapy. Each therapeutic modality engages the individual in a growth-oriented awareness process. The modalities range from reality orientation through an art and writing process (Art Therapy), to sensory-motor stimulation, integration and development (Occupational Therapy), to enacting and completing one's grieving process (Drama Therapy). The Expressive Therapy program is suited for a variety of individuals, including the nonverbal person, the person who has difficulty verbally and nonverbally expressing feelings and thoughts, those needing sensory-motor stimulation, and others with various physical and psychological disabilities and handicaps.

It is often difficult for individuals to discuss and deal with the physical and psychological disabilities accompanying aging. These issues may be brought up and discussed in a non-threatening manner through Expressive Therapy. This therapeutic process allows the individual to find a true sense of self in his activities, expressions, and personal experiences.

Category B, Psycho-Social Activity Program, includes activities which engage a person in group and individual experiences that stimulate and develop the psychological, sociological, and physical aspects of the individual. These activities can provide an invigorating group experience, promoting socialization and the development of personal skills through a well integrated, daily program. Examples of activities in this category are:

1. Active and passive group and individual games; indoor and outdoor activities and events; bedside leisure activities.
2. Extensive craft programs: learning new skills and continuing the use of skills already acquired.
3. Sheltered workshops: creating objects to sell; having a storefront, designed and managed by the participants, for the sale of craft items.
4. Weight awareness and pleasurable exercise program: instruction in nutrition for a weight program, and practicing yoga and Tai Chi for a pleasurable exercise program.
5. Swimming and jogging.
6. Dance classes: aerobic, folk, square dance, and other types of dancing.
7. Other activities and events which engage the psycho-social-physical aspects of the individual and enable the person to use his abilities to learn, be active, share, enjoy, and have fun.

Category C, Verbal Therapy (Group and Individual), provides counseling for elders and the disabled through the use of group and individual therapy, and discussion groups. Too often, in hospitals and institutions, therapy for elders and the disabled is largely concerned with the physical aspects of the individual. Counseling and psychotherapy is either minimal or is not provided in this setting.

Aging and disability not only physically hamper the individual but also beget psychological barriers, emotional traumas, phobias, and depression. These psychological injuries are often difficult to approach, deal with, and correct. The medical doctor aids in the healing of a person's body; but who is there to help heal the broken spirits and emotional losses, or to aid the individual to psychologically reorganize his or her life? In our society we may be afraid of disability, old age, and death, but our fears do not give us permission to disregard and avoid dealing with the problems of elders and the disabled.

Verbal therapy can aid elders and the disabled in dealing with their fears, depression, psychological barriers, and daily difficulties. Therapy sessions may be insight-oriented, analytical, or consciousness-raising discussions concerning personal conflicts, positive and negative stereotyping, or better ways of living and enjoying life. There are a variety of approaches a therapist can use (e.g., psychoanalytical, Gestalt, Rogerian) depending on the therapist's orientation and the receptivity of the client. Often, for elders and the disabled, group therapy can play an important role. Sharing feelings and thoughts with peers or with people who have a similar experience is a valuable process. Some appropriate themes and group designs are:

— men's or women's group, mixed group
— group with people who have a similar illness
— active reminiscence
— grieving process; saying goodbye and continuing your life
— self-esteem
— self-actualization; living your potential
— relaxation: body and mental relaxation; use of progressive muscle relaxation and visualization
— assertiveness
— drug and emotional dependence
— stress reduction
— dealing with daily life; problems and enjoyment.

Category D, Lifeskills Program, consists of short-term courses for learning lifeskills that are particularly useful and important in the client's daily life. A certificate should be given at the end of the successful completion of a course to promote feelings of self-esteem and accomplishment. Possible course topics are:

1. buying food, saving money with coupons, shopping carefully, and learning to cook new dishes
2. fixing household items that break
3. taking care of business, paying bills, budgeting money, and banking
4. learning to use the transportation system and going to new and interesting places
5. reading and writing
6. clothing coordination, mending clothes, cleaning clothes, and buying clothes
7. first aid and safety program
8. other skills needed by participants.

Category E, Cultural and Social Programs, encompasses activities that help people to be in touch with and participate in their cultural and social background. This may include attending cultural events, such as concerts, ballets, plays, food and movie festivals; or social programs such as religious occasions and holiday gatherings, political and educational lectures and movies, discussions, dances, and fairs.

Cultural and social programs are very important for elders and the disabled. It helps them to be socially active and feel that they are an important part of society and their culture. Too often elders and the disabled become socially isolated from their culture. This can foster frustration, resulting in depression and withdrawal from others. It is painful enough to experience the loss of family or close relations, or to live in a foreign environment without having the added burden of feeling like a social outcast.

Everyone needs an outlet, a stimulating event that brings new ideas and new experiences. This type of outlet can broaden a person's spectrum of cultural and social experiences and help to maintain the individual's involvement and interest in his or her social culture. Also, cultural and social events can help individuals focus their attention on positive experiences, diverting the critical self-reflection or depression that may often consume much of the aging and disabled person's life.

Category F, Homecare Program, focuses on people relating to their environment, designing and developing their surroundings to their own sensibilities, and having pride in their ability to add to their living space. The home or environment in which a person lives is a reflection of the individual. Feeling proud of one's living space often makes a person feel more comfortable and satisfied in his home.

Another aspect of Category F is dress and clothing care. The way a person dresses reflects his self-image. Awareness of dress and clothing care can add to the self-esteem and self-respect of the individual. Discussions on clothing styles and clothing care, with field trips to clothing stores, may provide a very enjoyable and educational activity.

In reference to homecare, the process of creating a pleasant environment can be a very nurturing activity. For example, taking care of a garden or a pet can be a very important aspect of a person's life. As people grow in age they often have a need or desire to help other things grow. An animal can often be very loving, receptive, and enjoyable to have and take care of. When an animal is not allowed in the home or living setting, plants, birds, or fish may be valuable substitutes. Field trips and group discussions on creating a home environment, interior decorating, caring for plants and animals, or acquiring new or used furniture and other household items are recommended.

A home is not just where a person sleeps but is an environment where the individual can create an enjoyable, comfortable, and self-rewarding place to live.

CONCLUSION

The six major categories of the Whole-Life Growth and Health Program provide a basic outline of services which meet many of the psychological, social, emotional, and physical needs of elders and the disabled. Although some facilities may not cover all six categories, they can supplement their programs with outside resources (e.g., consultants, therapists, and volunteers) and continue to develop their staff and in-house resources through in-service programs. The facility may also enhance client programs by providing educational benefits to the staff to support their study of therapeutic processes and programs which meet the needs of elders and the disabled.

The Whole-Life Growth and Health Program is based on a team approach and milieu therapy: everyone involved with the client works together in a supportive fashion. In this type of health-care system, a weekly team meeting to review the client's progress is vital. During these meetings the staff may discuss their various approaches, difficulties, and successes in working with clients, and suggest ways to upgrade the therapeutic programs of the individual and group. A major function of the staff is to work together to provide an effective integrated, depth-oriented therapeutic program for clients.

Working together implies a free and open exchange of communication between the staff. In this type of program the staff not only helps clients to become healthier, but as staff members give of themselves, they invigorate their own emotional and mental well-being. As staff members develop their individual therapeutic techniques, processes, and programs, they develop themselves. The staff is an integral part of the client's health, and need to grow with the client.

The Whole-Life Growth and Health Program has been created from seeing the needs of the elderly, of the disabled, of the weary and depressed who seem to have nowhere to turn and have difficulty communicating their needs. This program is also designed to reach, through a variety of therapeutic avenues, those who are classified as having no ability to progress, who are regressed or developmentally disabled, or seen as inept, unmanageable, chronic, and maintenance clients. This may include people who are seldom reached by our existing health-care system. The Whole-Life Growth and Health Program focuses on therapeutic processes that are tailored to meet the needs of clients who live in residential care, in long-term care, or who participate in day treatment programs.

A wholistic therapeutic program providing a variety of opportunities can be a crucial and valuable experience for clients. By developing a supportive, educational, and enlivening therapeutic program, the health-care milieu becomes a productive experience for everyone.

* * *

It is the author's opinion that no singular therapeutic technique or intervention, in itself, is the answer for treatment or aid for elders and the disabled, but rather a range of therapeutic experiences (with love) is needed. Some of the possible therapeutic processes to be used with elders and the disabled have been only briefly outlined. Further exploration and study of each therapeutic modality will be needed by the reader to appropriately use these techniques.

Whole-Life Growth and Health Program

Categories A, B, and C are therapeutic programs which focus on the psychological, sociological, and physical aspects of the individual. These programs aid the client by helping him work through problematic issues, gain a greater sense of self, and integrate a range of ego-supportive experiences.

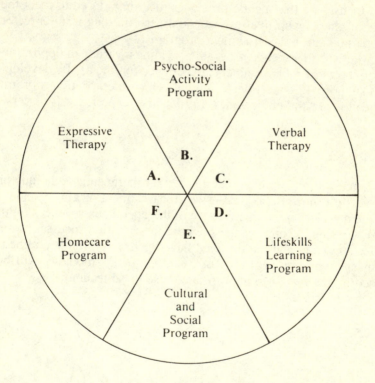

Categories D, E, and F are lifeskills programs which focus on meeting personal needs, learning new skills, self-care, and mental, physical, and social nourishment in a variety of daily life and program experiences.

Conclusion

PART I: THE SONG IS ONLY HEARD WHEN IT IS FELT

At times, when working as a therapist I asked myself: "If the client or patient were my father, mother, brother, or sister, would I offer the individual the same activities and opportunities in therapy?" Sometimes I put myself in the patient's place and questioned what I would want from the therapist. From my answer to this question, I reflected upon what I offered the patient. I found that by imagining myself in the patient's place, seeing through his eyes, talking to him about my experience, gave me a more empathetic and deeper understanding of his situation.

Often when working with disabled individuals, I realized that I could be that person; the only difference was that God allowed me to be where I was and the person to be where he was. In my work, I would thank the person for relating with me. I did not feel I was there only to help the patient; I felt that the patient was there to help me see him as he was. I came to feel we live in one world, and are brought together to learn, love, and grow.

As a therapist I try to reinforce an unconditional acceptance of the client from the vantage point of a deep respect for the individual. Of course, I do not condone all behavior, but I try to unconditionally relate to and accept a person for who he is, and what he is going through. I look for the beauty of the individual, the shining of the soul which has gone through many experiences. I feel that my acknowledgment of others helps them to see the beauty in themselves and gain a feeling of self-acceptance.

To speak of a creative therapeutic process that empowers a person with self-expression, understanding, and mature development is like trying to describe an ineffable growth process with words and ideas. The problem of communicating the full therapeutic process is related in the Tao thought:

> The Tao that can be told is not the eternal Tao. The name that can be named is not the eternal name.[1]

---

[1]Feng, G. F. and English, J. *Lao Tsu, Tao Te Ching.* New York: Random House, 1972, page 1.

The therapeutic process that is etched out only in words is one pattern of the process, devoid of the feeling, intensity, listening, communicative quality, and the client/therapist interaction. The true therapeutic process is an alive, responding, vibrant force between the client and therapist. I hope this process was communicated throughout the book.

PART II: GROWING OLD VS. OLD AND GROWING— UNIVERSITIES FOR THE SECOND PHASE OF LIFE

The process of growing old is a process of life; of giving and receiving, of metamorphosis and growth. If we do not allow our lives to change, we may never begin to see the newness of each and every moment. If we do not know what it means to "relax" ourselves from living in the past and join the present, we will fixate and crystallize an image of ourselves and others that is extraneous to the present reality. Young people grow old with an emphasis on old. Growing old when young has positive connotations. There are challenges to be met, friends to be made, and a world to explore. Growing old for an elder can have the same positive connotations. The real challenge is to use the skills and resources gathered throughout a lifetime to daily enhance one's life.

The concept and fact of growing old in our society has connotations of a lack of dignity, almost of disgrace (i.e., some people are afraid to tell their age because they fear someone would think less of them if they are at a certain age, the age of being "old"). Life for people who feel negatively about aging is often a narcissistic encounter. They are continually trying to save face, be youthful, forget tomorrow, and "save" themselves from the truth of their aging life.

In our culture, aging and approaching death is seen as a negative concept instead of a fulfillment of one's life. The fear of death can keep people from being true to their feelings and true to their life. This fear can also prevent people from taking the opportunity to cherish the moment. To live in fear of death is a stifling experience. To live with the recognition of death can often alert a person to the value of the moment.

Approaching death can be seen as a form of personal growth. Like a flower that looses its petals as it grows into a larger plant, life is a continual process of maturation and growth. Over the years, a person may wear down his physical body but refines his "inner soul" through life experiences. This refining takes much conscious work, understanding, and experience in life.

Although the physical body and, possibly, the mental and/or motor functions of the individual may lessen with age, each person had other faculties which may compensate for that loss. We need to take advantage of our abilities and not forget to use and keep our mind and body in shape. What you don't use, you lose!

Senior citizen centers and apartment complexes, retirement communities, nursing homes, adult day care programs, hospitals, and long-term care institutions for the elderly and disabled can be the "Universities" for the second phase of life.

> I said just now that we have no schools for forty-year-olds. That is not true. Our religions were always such schools in the past, but how many people regard them like that today? How many of us older ones have been brought up in such a school and really prepared for the second half of life, for old age, death, and eternity?[2]

These "Universities" should be places where a person can revitalize his emotional, intellectual, physical, and spiritual well-being—a place where the individual can share his wisdom and abilities and be able to give and receive love; a place where an individual can learn to have a clearer understanding of life through reflecting upon, expressing, creating, and acknowledging life. The world is our school and if we choose we will never stop learning and growing.

PART III: CREATIVE EXPRESSION

Creative expression is one of the clearest self-directed reflections of a person's life. Through the creative process, the individual speaks in a language that is so deep and meaningful that, at times, there are no words to express it. The sounds and colors a person creates vividly reflects the inner self. The exploration of the creative process (in art, music, movement poetry, drama, etc.) enables the individual to experience a daily fruition of self-expression and un-

[2]Campbell, J. (ed.) *The Portable Jung.* New York: The Viking Press, Inc., 1971, page 17.

derstanding. It can give a deeper meaning to a person's life and provide an outlet for one's feelings and thoughts.

Creativity is not just painting, sculpting, writing, or dancing; it is a way of creating and joining in life that gives significance to a person's inner and social experiences. The individual is the creative sculptor of his life. The final sculpture is himself and his life, which is an expression of the refinement of his experiences, knowledge, understanding, and love.

A person's life experiences are like waves of the sea: pounding, caressing, smoothing, refining the rocks by the shore. The basic form of the rocks may never change, but the rocks always change in subtle ways. A person's fortitude is like the solid aspect of the rock, and one's character and self-expression are the subtle sculpting, changing, and molding of oneself through experiences and understanding: the metamorphic rock.

Expressive therapy uses one's experiences, feelings, intuitions, and understanding as self-directed tools for clarifying and recognizing the beauty and love in life. In this process a person comes to feel and see what he already has in life, not just what he thinks he wants. Some people search for the truth and beauty in life, and some participate in life to the fullest and uncover the truth, and are the beauty.

Have you seen a person die?
I have seen the hands of death take away the breath of life.
Do you know what it means to live?
Not just to exist or survive, but to live from your dreams, your potential, from the sweat of your brow and the strength of your hands.
Do you realize what it is to create?
It is like a fountain of energy flowing through you. It inspires you, it enlivens you, it loves you, and it heals you.
Do you know that our daily life is our creation?

PART IV: MORNING FOLLOWS EVERY NIGHT

During my work in an institutional setting the staff did not expect any enthusiastic creative response from the elderly and disabled patients. The doctors, nurses, and orderlies told me that the patients were too nonresponsive and confused to participate in art therapy. They were pleasantly surprised when I hung the patients' drawings and paintings on the wall.

The patients had become enlivened by their new experience of creating so much art and activity that they began to exhibit a new personal freedom in expressing themselves and relating to others. Here, a true therapeutic, interactive milieu manifested because patients were able to express themselves in ways that were not usually available to them due to inhibiting social norms and the hospital atmosphere.

Creative expression and expressive therapy allowed patients to discover an outlet and the means to find, express, and clarify their thoughts and feelings. It gave them a chance to discuss, in a group setting with other patients, their feelings about the hospital, their losses and happiness in life. The creative process gave patients an impetus to see a new depth and meaning in life that some had previously overlooked, denied, or not encountered. It gave patients a chance to face their life and feelings of death, to reconcile their strong and weak moments, their trials and tribulations, and to help them gain an ability to master a healthy perspective in living.

The results of the expressive therapy sessions astonished me because of the positive effects they had on the group process and individual dynamics. I saw people reaching out to others, sparking off feelings of warmth, closeness, and a sense of community. Individuals who said they were blind, focused their eyes and read what they wrote; those who said they couldn't hear, sang along; and those who were completely withdrawn reached out to others. Until then, I never fully realized there was so much untapped potential just waiting to be released.

My major task as the group therapist was to be a facilitator—to give the participants an opportunity, an inspiration to share themselves, with an unconditional acceptance for whatever they chose to share verbally or nonverbally. In our camaraderie we needed to be felt and heard by each other. I found this type of relationship with my group very rewarding.

This book reflects only a portion of the untold potential of elders and the disabled. The descriptions, stories, and concepts in this book are only words which emphasize the importance of a person's creative expression and the value expressive therapy can play in assisting elders and the disabled in sharing, clarifying, and enlightening their lives. For the person who truly engages in life there are new and exciting beginnings.

To reflect, experience, share, and to know oneself is one of the greatest joys in life; being at peace with one's life journey.

PART V: A RITE OF PASSAGE

As the years pass on for the elderly and disabled individual, something miraculous happens at times. The person may experience a new perspective in reviewing his life. He begins to have a sense of what it means to complete his life. It may be a time when the individual faces his own mortality, or the way his life actually is, and he begins to let go of his anger, frustration, and resistance toward life. At those moments the individual may also let go of negative and ineffective patterns of behavior and thought. He begins to embrace life, to let down his guard, and to reach out to other people. This is a time when his life can embody a new found truth, beauty, and grace with which to receive others. It is at this moment the individual opens his arms to life; to feelings of love and wishes for the best to be in everyone's life.

This type of transformation may be scary for people who are not ready to face the fact that one day they must complete their life. Often people live in a dream of immortality, holding onto the past, with a tremendous fear of the pains of life. It is this fear which gives the individual the most pain. It is the running away from sadness or loss which makes a person so scared. But for the individual who is consciously aware of completing his life, it is a beautiful experience. It is a time to see one's life in a new light; for the individual to take account of his experiences—the blessings and tragedies. This experience has many feelings, those of happiness, sadness, longing, and loving. It touches the heart of life.

The present is the only time a person has to feel, share, and act. The only time to be, the way you want to be, is now: to speak of your heart and to touch the heart of life.

BIBLIOGRAPHY

Campbell, J. (ed.) *The Portable Jung.* New York: The Viking Press, Inc., 1971.
Feng, G. F. and English, J. *Lao Tsu, Tao Te Ching.* New York: Random House, 1972.

Appendix

CHARTING THE CREATIVE ARTS THERAPY EXPERIENCE

Charting is the act of noting the distinct steps a client takes within a therapeutic program. The therapist may often discover new directions in the client's treatment and activity during this notation and review process. The insight gained by seeing a client's picture, drawing, or statement in relation to the total case can guide the therapist in clarifying therapeutic issues and enhancing the therapist's understanding of a problem area.

One major reason for charting is to note a client's development, signifying the areas of need and growth in a direct, efficient manner. Charting also conveys the response of a client toward a particular treatment modality in reference to the usefulness of the modality and the progress of the client. Charting creative arts and creative arts therapy sessions is very helpful to the treatment team in gaining insight into the individual and group dynamics. Through this process, the individual activities, group involvement, and the emotional and cognitive expressions and explorations of each client are noted.

To effectively chart a client's participation and note progress in creative arts therapy sessions I have developed two forms: the "Client Individual/Group Session" (see page 209) and the "Creative Arts Group Process" (see page 210). The "Client Individual/ Group Session" form is for noting the client's psycho-social responses within the session. The "Creative Arts Group Process" form is designed as a basic form for charting the major outline of the activity, the dynamics of the participants and possible future group projects or therapeutic interventions. Often therapists do not have time to write in-depth essays on clients after each session, therefore these forms can be used by the therapist or health-care worker to concisely point out significant issues or material from the session.

An additional form "Basic Background Information on Client" (see page 208), is designed for obtaining a profile of the individual's personal history. This form would be kept as a reference with the creative arts therapy charting. Important areas covered by this form are:

Diagnosis – a medical or psychological diagnosis as noted in the client's medical record by a licensed therapist or physician.

Medical information/Doctor – refers to the client's physical health, health-related problems or difficulties, and notes the name of the client's doctor.

Medications – listed due to the significant psychological and physical effect they can have on the individual.

Physical limitations – noted to cite physical needs and difficulties the individual may have.

Previous or current occupations – listed to aid the therapist gain insight into the participant's background.

Interests and hobbies – to give a broad view of the participant's enjoyment in activities and leisure time which may provide a vehicle for further personal growth.

Goals in therapy – to signify the participant's personal needs and wants in therapy.

Goals in life – to indicate what the participant feels is most important to strive for in his life.

Other information – to note significant material which has not already been listed that may aid toward a greater understanding of the participant, such as his needs, desires, wishes, limitations, frustrations, abilities, social-economic influences, religious background, and other items.

In the "Client Individual/Group Session" form (see page 209), Section I is an overview of the client's participation in an activity. This section is for noting the *activity,* the *length of time in the activity and discussion,* the participant's *feelings about the activity,* and other items. *Positive aspects and problems or conflicts for the participant within the activity* are both listed to give a closer view of the participant's involvement in the activity. *Future therapeutic intervention* is also noted in Section I. This is a general statement by the therapist and/or client about issues or therapeutic interventions the client may wish or need to explore.

Section II points to more specific aspects of the client's involvement in the session. Areas covered are:

Participation level (active/passive) – noting the amount and type of group or individual participation in the activity.

Cognitive process – signifies the individual's cognitive abilities and expressions during the activity.

Motor ability – refers to the capacity to use one's body (arms, hands, fingers, etc. . . .) in the activity.

Sensory ability – refers to the capability to relate and use one's senses such as taste, touch, hearing, seeing, and smelling.

Range and depth of emotional expression – refers to the degree of the client's self-expression and exploration within the session.

Section III, *Creative Arts Expression/Media* deals specifically with charting the art or craft activity. *Media* signifies the art medium used in the session. If drawing, painting, or sculpting is done by the participant, then *Color* and *Line* should be described. *Theme* refers to the major idea or focus of the art expression. Other areas covered in this section are:

Spatial arrangement, configuration – for designating the pattern of the design or picture in relation to its boundaries (the paper, canvas, or sculpture area) and itself.

Client's and/or therapist's interpretation of expression – for noting the client's or therapist's meaning of the art expression in relation to the client's feelings, thoughts, and actions. For example, this would be an appropriate place to note the client's cathartic release of energy within the session, the sublimation of thoughts and feelings onto an art piece, or the affect and verbal expression of a client after he or she has completed an art piece.

The "Creative Arts Group Process" form (see page 210) is designed for the therapist or health-care worker who wants to outline the basic group experience. It is a short form to highlight the major events in the session. Listed below the heading of this form are: *Theme/Project; Date;* and *Therapist/Group Leader.* Next listed are the *Participants* in the group and their *Activity.* Under the activity section the therapist or health-care worker can describe the participants' group or individual creative arts activity.

Listed next on the "Creative Arts Group Process" form is *Interaction* for the therapist to note and describe the individual or group interactional process in the activity. The form concludes with *Possible future group projects or therapeutic interventions* followed by *Other information.* This area is for the therapist to describe his ideas which stemmed from the session, such as projects or interventions to be used in future group or individual sessions and any other pertinent information.

The "Client Individual/Group Session" and the "Creative Arts Group Process" forms are designed to enable the therapist to outline carefully the therapeutic process and experience of the client and group for documentation and periodic review. These forms do not totally describe the creative experience of the individual, but rather point out significant factors within the session. Further documentation of the therapist's process within the group or creative activity may also be helpful. The charting forms should be adjusted to the needs of each health-care facility. This type of documentation can help the professional and paraprofessional health-care worker in maintaining a clear and concise record of creative arts therapy sessions and the client's participation in activities.

Basic Background Information on Client

Name _____   Date _____

Diagnosis _____   Age & birthdate _____

_____

Medical info./Doctor _____

_____

Medications _____

_____

Physical limitations _____

_____

Previous or current occupation _____

_____

Interests and hobbies _____

_____

Goals in therapy _____

_____

Goals in life _____

_____

Other information _____

_____

_____

_____

Client Individual/Group Session

Name _____ Date _____

Therapist/Group Leader _____

Section I: Activity _____

Length of time in activity and discussion _____

Feelings about the activity (affect) _____

Positive aspects of client in the activity _____

Problems or conflicts in the activity _____

Future therapeutic interventions _____

_____

Section II: Participation level (active/passive) _____

Cognitive level _____

Motor ability _____

Sensory ability _____

Range and depth of emotional expression _____

Section III: Creative arts expression/media _____

Theme _____

Color _____

Line _____

Spatial arrangement/configuration _____

Client's and/or therapist's interpretation of expression ____

_____

_____

Creative Arts Group Process

Theme/Project: _____   Date _____
_____   Therapist/Group Leader _____

Participants   Activity

_____   _____
_____   _____
_____   _____
_____   _____
_____   _____
_____   _____
_____   _____
_____   _____
_____   _____
_____   _____
_____   _____

Interaction

_____
_____
_____
_____
_____
_____

Possible future group projects or therapeutic intervention

_____
_____
_____
_____
_____
_____

Other information

_____
_____

Index

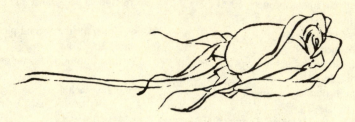

The greatest art we create is our life.